The Philosophy Of Ibn Arabi - Primary Source Edition

Landau, Rom.

ETHICAL AND RELIGIOUS CLASSICS

OF EAST AND WEST

NO 22

THE PHILOSOPHY OF IBN 'ARABĪ

ETHICAL AND RELIGIOUS CLASSICS OF EAST AND WEST

---

1. *Reynold A. Nicholson:* RŪMĪ: POET AND MYSTIC
2. *A. J. Arberry:* SUFISM
3. *Arthur Waley:* THE POETRY AND CAREER OF LI PO
4. *George Kaftal:* SAINT FRANCIS IN ITALIAN PAINTING
5. *E. Allison Peers:* THE MYSTICS OF SPAIN
6. *Dastur Bode* and *Piloo Nanavutty:* SONGS OF ZARATHUSTRA
7. *Emmy Wellesz:* AKBAR'S RELIGIOUS THOUGHT
8. *W. Montgomery Watt:* THE FAITH AND PRACTICE OF AL-GHAZĀLĪ
9. *A. J. Arberry:* THE HOLY KORAN
10. *A. H. Armstrong:* PLOTINUS
11. *Israel Mattuck:* THE THOUGHT OF THE PROPHETS
12. *Leon Roth:* GOD AND MAN IN THE OLD TESTAMENT
13. *Edward Conze:* BUDDHIST MEDITATION
14. *R. C. Zachner:* THE TEACHINGS OF THE MAGI
15. *D. M. Lang:* LIVES AND LEGENDS OF THE GEORGIAN SAINTS
16. *Kaizuka:* CONFUCIUS
17. *F. H. Hilliard:* THE BUDDHA, THE PROPHET AND THE CHRIST
18. *W. G. Archer:* THE LOVES OF KRISHNA
19. *Kātib Chelebi:* THE BALANCE OF TRUTH
20. *D. M. Lang:* THE WISDOM OF BALAHVAR
21. *F. Rahman:* PROPHECY IN ISLAM

THE PHILOSOPHY OF IBN 'ARABĪ

by

ROM LANDAU

RUSKIN HOUSE
GEORGE ALLEN & UNWIN LTD
MUSEUM STREET LONDON

First published in 1959

Printed in Great Britain
in 11 on 12 pt. Baskerville type
by C. Tinling & Co. Ltd.
Liverpool, London and Prescot.

PREFACE

Ibn 'Arabī is possibly the most significant thinker of Islam. Yet he is far less widely known in the Western world than Ibn Sīnā, Al-Ghazālī, Ibn Rushd or even Al-Fārābī. By and large, the legend of his pantheism and his obscurity persists in a world little aware of what he actually wrote and taught. The late R. A. Nicholson and Dr. A. E. Affifi are the English-speaking world's chief contribution to Ibn 'Arabī studies. The present essay attempts to fill, however inadequately, the gap that remains. It touches only upon some of the main ideas in Ibn 'Arabī's vast and complex system, and ignores innumerable other aspects. Apart from my own interpretations and illustrations of some of Ibn 'Arabī's puzzling ideas, I do not claim any special originality for this study. I hope, nevertheless, that even so concise an introduction to him might offer some notion of his philosophy, and induce the reader to seek out the original sources. For the sake of those unable to read Ibn 'Arabī in the original, I have included a number of his texts in English.

Apart from Ibn 'Arabī's own writings, especially the *Fuṣūṣ* and the *Futūḥāt*, the chief authorities on whom I have based my text are Miguel Asin y Palacios, R. A. Nicholson, and, especially, Dr. Affifi, whose book, *The Mystical Philosophy of Muḥyīd Dīn-Ibnul 'Arabī* (Cambridge University Press, 1939) might well claim to be the clearest survey in English of a difficult but fascinating subject.

ROM LANDAU,
Professor of Islamics,
North African Studies,
College of the Pacific,
California.

ACKNOWLEDGEMENTS

I wish to express my gratitude to the following publishers for giving me permission to use translations of Ibn 'Arabī texts: the University Press Cambridge (*Studies in Islamic Mysticism*, by Reynold Alleyne Nicholson, publ. 1921), the Royal Asiatic Society, London (*Tarjumānu 'l-Ashwāq*, by Reynold A. Nicholson, publ. 1911), and Messrs Luzac & Co. London (*Readings from the Mystics of Islam*, publ. 1950). I also have to thank the Editors of *The Muslim World*, Hartford Seminary Foundation, Hartford, Conn. for allowing me to use material contained in my *The Philosophy of Ibn 'Arabi*, published in January and April 1957 in their Quarterly.

CONTENTS

PART ONE

ONE

THE LIFE OF IBN ʿARABĪ

Abū Bakr Muḥammad ibn ʿAlī Muḥyī al-Dīn al-Ḥātimī al Andalusī, commonly known as Ibn ʿArabī (or Ibnul ʿArabī), came from a pious family in which Ṣūfī interests were a tradition. His ancestors belonged to the Arab tribe of Tayy. At some time or another they moved from the Middle East to Southern Spain which, from the beginning of the 8th century, had been ruled by Arabian princes. By A.D. 1164, when Ibn ʿArabī was born in Murcia, in South-Eastern Spain, Muslim dominance in the Iberian peninsula had passed its peak and, indeed, was declining towards extinction. But Spanish intellectual life was still illumined by the after-glow of Moorish civilization. During the preceding three centuries, the intellectual zest and material splendour of Cordova and Seville surpassed those of Paris and possibly even of Constantinople. The Muslims of Spain had transmitted to Europe much of the wisdom of the Greeks; and with their co-religionists in Syria, Persia and Iraq had produced a corpus of philosophical and scientific knowledge that was to leave a deeper imprint upon European civilization than any other foreign culture, before or since.

At the beginning of the 12th century, an Arab youth in Andalusia had practically the whole of the then available knowledge spread before him in the schools and libraries of Southern Spain. Zoroastrian and Manichaean lore, Hebrew and Christian theology, Greek philosophy and mathematics, and every kind of

Muslim intellectual achievement were by then formulated in manuscript, and there was no dearth of scholars to expound. It seems that Ibn 'Arabī, with his exceptional spiritual curiosity grasped every opportunity to profit from all available sources. At the age of eight he was in Lisbon where he received the rudiments of Muslim orthodox education. Besides learning the Qur'ān, he studied the principles of Islamic law. A few years later we find him in Seville, since 1170 the capital of the Moorish Empire of the Almohades. He remained there for some thirty years, continually employed in the study of the various branches of Islamic learning. During that time he also travelled extensively in both Spain and Morocco, and, in 1201, decided to make the pilgrimage to Mecca. He may have sought thus to escape from the simmering political upheavals in Spain and from the vigilant eyes of the learned *ulema*, who would look askance at a Ṣūfī scholar of distinctly unorthodox views. In the East, he visited not only Mecca, where he lived and taught for a while, but also Syria, Iraq and Asia Minor. By that time, his saintly life and his impressive record as a teacher and thinker had earned him great renown. Wherever he went, gifts were bestowed upon him, which later he passed on to the poor.

It was during his sojourn in Mecca and Damascus that Ibn 'Arabi wrote most of his books, especially the fundamental *Fuṣūṣu 'l-Ḥikam*, known in English as either *Gems of Philosophy* or *The Bezels of Divine Wisdom*, and *Al Futūḥāt al-Makkiyyah* (*Meccan Revelations*). We have no exact knowledge of the number of books he wrote. He himself mentions almost three hundred. These comprise theology, mysticism, biography, philosophy, Quranic commentaries, and poetry. Ibn 'Arabī died in 1240 in Damascus, where his grave can be seen to the present day.

TWO

IBN 'ARABĪ AND ISLAMIC PHILOSOPHY

THE central problem facing the Muslim philosophers was how to reconcile a God of absolute unity and perfection with the creation of a multiple universe full of imperfections. If God's *will* was responsible for the creation of the world, then we are confronted with the problem of the duality of God and His will. The same problem arises in regard to Divine mercy, charity, justice and the other attributes of God. Then there was the problem how the postulate of God's unity could be preserved in view of the fact that some 'part' of Him became the universe. Prior to the creation of the latter there was nothing beside God. So obviously the universe must be a 'fragment' of God's being, taken out of eternity and placed into time. Since God is eternal and spiritual, He must be beyond time, space and matter. Yet what distinguishes His universe from Himself is precisely its material existence in time and space. Whence did these come, with all their multiplicity and imperfections?

These problems had worried not merely the Muslim philosophers but also their antecedents and masters, the Greeks, from Aristotle down to Philo, Plotinus and Origen. Though the Muslims accepted many of the Aristotelian and Neo-platonic postulates, they did not develop them merely as Muslim interpretations. Each thinker attempted clarification in his own individual way. Hardly any two of them re-expressed the doctrine of the *Nous* or of the *Logos* in identical manner, each seeking a formula that would, to his mind, satisfy the demands of logic and yet not contravene the doctrines of the Qur'ān. Their interpretations ranged from the rationalism of the Mu'tazilah to the intellectual sterility of the Ash'arites; from unredeemed anthropomorphism to the complex doctrine of world spirits as postulated by Ibn Sīnā; from Al-Fārābī's veneration of Aristotelian mathematics and astronomy to Al-Ghazālī's revolt against both the Greeks and philosophy *sui generis.*

Some of the schemes devised by the Muslim philosophers are eminently satisfying to the demands of logic. They have the beauty of true works of art. By interposing an active 'agent' between God and His creation —whether called Universal Reason or First Cause, *Logos* or Universal Spirit—they relieved God of all responsibility for the existence of such troublesome entities as time, space, multiplicity, and so on. But when, at the beginning of the 12th century, Al-Ghazālī wrote his *Tahāfut al-Falāsifah* he showed that his predecessors, despite the apparent impeccability of their reasoning, had shirked the central issue. Their solutions had been essentially linguistic ones. By substituting the term Divine 'knowledge' for Divine 'will', and the Neoplatonic 'necessity' for 'creation', they imagined themselves to have overcome all the difficulties. They had made the universe finite in space and infinite in duration; they had limited God (or, rather, the First Cause) to dealing only with universals and not with particulars; they had attributed to everything an eternal potential existence (in the mind of God) and had thus eliminated the 'possibility' of anything new being created by God, for such new creation would have removed God from eternity and placed Him in time. Not so, insisted Al-Ghazālī, opposing such mental acrobatics. Even God's thinking must be the outcome of His will. Since He knows everything He must be concerned not only with universals but also with particulars. How, he challenged his predecessors, could we conceive of a finite space and an infinite time? Does not infinite time presuppose also infinite space? Is not space related to body, and time to the body's movement? And, Al-Ghazālī, a more orthodox Muslim than they, protested that not only the soul, as the philosophers said, but also the body is immortal. Though the great Ibn Rushd wrote his scathing *Tahāfut al-Tahāfut* against Al-Ghazālī, and used every weapon of Aristotelian logic against him, he did not really invalidate Al-Ghazālī's arguments. But the verbal ingenuities he employed proved sufficiently persuasive to influence Western scholastics for several centuries.

The Muslim philosophers accomplished their tasks efficiently. Their efforts compare by no means unfavourably with those of some of their great successors, such as Descartes, Kant or Leibniz. Kant's *Das Ding an sich* added little to the *shay'* (thing) of the Muslims; and the monad of Leibniz can hardly claim superiority over its cousin, the atom of Muslim atomists. It must, however, be conceded that the Muslim philosophers failed to resolve the fundamental conflict between the Qur'ān and its *rational* justification, just as the Western scholastics failed to solve the corresponding conflict in the Christian doctrine. The fault, however, was not theirs. It was inherent in the conflict itself. The fundamental truths of the Qur'ān, in common with those of all genuine religions, are spiritual truths. Their postulates and their 'logic' must needs differ from those that have formed the basis of Western philosophical (and scientific) pursuits ever since Aristotle. It may be that the truths of science and of rationalism in general pose no insoluble riddles to Aristotelian logic, though it would appear that modern atomic science and mathematics are beginning to find them insufficient. In dealing, however, with dimensions of truth in which matter (and substance) are not the one and all, we find that particular logic of little assistance. Whether we accept or dismiss the truths of mysticism, we all agree that those truths cannot be 'proved' by a logic derived essentially from Aristotle. Such logic bases itself on a quantitative universe in which substance, whether in the sense of *materia prima* or *materia secunda* is the decisive reality of existence. By disregarding quality—which it attempts to define in terms of quantity—it takes little heed of essence. The underlying forces behind the universe—the instruments of the First Cause, or God, or whatever we wish to call it—are, however, timeless and spaceless essence. Quantity does not enter therein, even though it may become a vehicle. Thus, in trying to explain essence in terms of substance—the common technique of most Western philosophy—we attempt to explain one dimension by another one.

The problems awaiting solution by the Muslim philosophers were beyond the power of the Aristotelian logic that most of them accepted. Evidently a less circumscribed, a more 'spiritual', instrument was needed. The mystics alone appear to have possessed such an instrument, which we might describe as vision—a direct awareness of Reality, unencumbered by intellectual interference. Though it might not be impossible to arrive at similar truths by intellectual means, such findings will be only accidental, and they will have been gained at second hand. While they reach us after having been distilled through, or reflected in, our intellect, the truths obtained by direct vision are an immediate and spontaneous experience. We might liken them to light reaching us direct from the sun as compared with light depicted in an artist's painting. (Since the great artist, somewhat like the mystic, *sees* truth directly, his representation of truth will be more concrete than that of the scientist.)

THREE

THE NATURE OF IBN 'ARABĪ'S DOCTRINE

THE truths expressed in the philosophy of Ibn 'Arabī are those of a seer and a mystic, not of a philosopher, even though he did his best to explain them through a philosophical system. His uniqueness derives precisely from the fact that he was both a seer—who often saw more clearly and more deeply even than other mystics—and at the same time possessed the equipment of a philosopher, however unorthodox and even fantastic that equipment appears at times to have been.

Though the core of his doctrine and many of its details are Ibn 'Arabī's own, his vast reading and his catholicity enabled him to utilize innumerable extraneous sources. Of the purely native, or Spanish sources, most prominent were those of the Ṣūfīs of Al-Meria, whose doctrines spread through most of Muslim Spain. In his book on our philosopher, however, Dr A. E. Affifi shows that the influence of the Spanish Ṣūfī, Ibn Masarra, and his schools, affected Ibn 'Arabī far less than was assumed by the great Spanish expert, Miguel Asin y Palacios. The Qur'ān and Ḥadīth form the chief basis upon which Ibn 'Arabī builds his doctrine. That he would be influenced by his pantheistic predecessor, the martyred Al-Ḥallāj, goes without saying. The same is true of several Eastern Ṣūfīs with whose work Ibn 'Arabī became acquainted during his stay in the Middle East. Coming after most of the founders of Islamic scholasticism, he naturally derived a great deal from the Ash'arites, the Mu'tazilah, the Carmathians and the

Ikhwān al-Ṣafā, the earliest Muslim encyclopaedists Aristotle, in the Neo-platonic garb provided for him by the Muslim philosophers, left profound traces in Ibn 'Arabī's system. So did the Hellenistic schools of Plotinus and the Stoics. Scholars have also detected Zoroastrian and Manichaean influences. Yet, whatever his source, he seldom failed to assimilate it so completely as to make it appear to originate in his own mind. This is particularly true of the use he makes of the Qur'ān which he interprets in any way that happens to suit his peculiarly uncompromising system.

Ibn 'Arabī's philosophy is usually described as pantheistic. Pantheism however, as commonly understood, is little more than an ennobled form of materialism. Only in recent years have scholars begun to call Ibn 'Arabī a monist. Yet the term monism, as applied to him, seems not sufficiently qualitative to provide an adequate label for the great Murcian's theosophy. The term that might possibly suit his doctrine best is non-dualism, a term that implies not merely its monistic character but also its complete overcoming of all dualistic conceptions. He is, indeed, the sole Muslim thinker who, while accepting the uncompromising monotheism of the Qur'ān, succeeded in providing that gospel with a philosophical interpretation that resolves the innumerable problems of duality as implied by the seemingly mutually contradictory statements of Islam's holy text.

If it can be said that one single consideration preoccupied Ibn 'Arabī more than any other it was the necessity for proving the non-duality of everything concerning God and His universe. A purely monistic answer to the problems of the apparent duality of a perfect God and an imperfect universe, of active and passive, of good and evil, of Divine omnipotence and human free will, would not have sufficed. It had to be shown unmistakably that there was no room for any duality whatsoever within and between the various elements. If any Western philosopher, rooted in a Semitic *Weltanschauung*, succeeded in providing such a non-dualistic philosophy, it was Ibn 'Arabī. He may often strain our patience almost beyond endurance; he may tax our powers of comprehension more severely than any other philosopher, Western or Eastern; his apparent ambiguities and contradictions may drive us wellnigh to despair. But finally our patience is richly rewarded. A splendid system of perfect non-dualism rises before us, and innumerable questions that other Western systems leave only partially explained receive answers equally satisfying from a philosophical and a religious point of view.

The difficulties which Ibn 'Arabī presents to the student lie not so much in the doctrine itself as in his style and method of reasoning. Some of these complexities are deliberate; others derive from his peculiar type of mind. Conscious of the dangers threatening an unorthodox thinker setting his views against those of theologians representing authority, Ibn 'Arabī deliberately complicated his style. He would try to make an outrageously heterodox piece of argumentation look irreproachable by expressing it in the language or imagery of orthodoxy. An original but not a systematic philosopher, he did not hesitate to use the same term to denote a number of different ideas, or to use identical terms to describe ideas that were not only not identical but mutually contradictory. A poet as well as a philosopher, he might employ a poetical diction that would pass muster in a lyrical work but only served to make his argument abtruse or even suggested an essential lack of self-discipline. As no single book contains his philosophy *in toto*, and his doctrine is to be extracted laboriously from the gargantuan volumes of the *Futūḥāt* and the *Fuṣūṣ*—not to speak of a number of less prolix books—it will be evident that the task of commentators is not easy. Only a very genuine admiration of that remarkable genius can induce a student to wrangle with the innumerable difficulties that Ibn ʿArabī found it necessary to create.

Yet he has fascinated thinkers, theologians and poets almost from the day his works became known.

It was inevitable that countless orthodox theologians should be revolted by what appeared heterodox, even scandalous in the ways in which he interpreted Qur'ānic doctrine. His views on the incarnation of God in man (*hulūl*) or the identification of man with God (*ittiḥād*) were naturally anathema to them. For is not the utter absence of such an incarnation one of Islam's fundamental postulates, one that distinguishes it so proudly from Christian 'polytheism'? The learned *ulema*, of course, did not perceive that Ibn ʿArabī's doctrine of incarnation had nothing in common with the orthodox interpretation of the concept of incarnation. Throughout the centuries, controversy over Ibn ʿArabī continued whenever his name was mentioned in theological or philosophical gatherings. Yet even his most ardent partisans—and they were legion—admitted that mystical doctrines as profound and as blindingly illuminating as his represented a danger to anyone but the initiated. Nevertheless, Muslim scholars persevered in reading his writings, and many a Ṣūfī would copy these if only, by so doing, he might secure the blessing of their author. Among the better known scholars who defended his views we find Majdu 'l-Dīn al-Fīrūzābādī (died A.D. 1414), Jalālu 'l-Dīn al-Suyūṭī (d. 1445), and, a century later, ʿAbdu 'l-Wahhāb al-Shaʿrānī.

In the Western world, Dante provides one of the most conspicuous examples of Ibn 'Arabī's pervasive influence. Señor Asin y Palacios, the leading authority on the subject, has proved in his remarkable studies published in the volume *Islam and the Divine Comedy* (John Murray, London, 1926) that not only were innumerable ideas in the *Divine Comedy* inspired by Ibn 'Arabī, but the entire geography of heaven and hell was taken over by Dante from Ibn 'Arabī (and other Muslim sources). And to mention but one other Western thinker whose work unmistakably shows Ibn 'Arabī's influence, there is Ramon Lull, the Spanish mystic.

FOUR

THEMES IN IBN 'ARABĪ'S PHILOSOPHY

(A) GOD

IF Ibn 'Arabī is usually described as a pantheist, there is ample justification in his own arguments. For while the Qur'ān declares: 'There is but one God', Ibn 'Arabī maintains that 'there is nothing but God'. His abandonment of the Islamic conception of God as the creator and cause of the universe, in favour of a God who *is* everything, definitely suggests a step from monotheism to pantheism. While the Prophet Muḥammad preached a God who is cause and a universe that is effect, the majority of Muslim philosophers introduced between God and His creation such intermediaries as the First Cause or the Universal Spirit. Ibn 'Arabī will have none of these intermediaries, but only 'absolute unification'. Though again and again he tries to reconcile his 'pantheistic' God with the unitarian God of the Qur'ān, his God 'Who is everything' must needs differ greatly from the Quranic God 'like unto whom there is nothing'. His God is not one who creates or from whom anything but Himself emanates, but a God who *manifests* Himself in an infinity of forms.

Ibn 'Arabī distinguishes between the finite God of religion and the infinite God of mysticism. The God of religion reveals Himself in various forms reflected in the different religions. It depends upon the 'capacity' of the believer which one of these forms (religions) he accepts. The God of the mystic contains all His forms, for the mystic's heart alone is all-receptive. While the

God of religion manifests Himself in man as both virtue and sin, the God of the mystic reveals Himself in a manner that is beyond virtue and sin. As we shall discover, this is an utterly a-moral God.

That the mystic's God can obviously be neither Muslim nor Christian, Buddhist, Jewish nor pagan is expressed beautifully in Ibn 'Arabi's famous ode contained in his *Tarjumānu 'l-Ashwāq*, a collection of mystical odes:

> 'My heart is capable of every form,
> A cloister for the monk, a fane for idols,
> A pasture for gazelles, the pilgrim's Ka'ba,
> The Tables of the Torah, the Koran.
> Love is the faith I hold: wherever turn
> His camels, still the one true faith is mine.'[1]

Since God is the essence of all existence, man needs Him so that he may exist. On the other hand, God needs man, so that He may manifest Himself to Himself.

Divine essence, for Ibn 'Arabī, is pure without attributes. It is endowed with Attributes when it manifests itself, either in the universe or in man (who is part of it), for all created things are His Attributes. Viewed as His Attributes, they are identical with God. When viewed *apart* from God—as they are by the rationalist and materialist—they are nothing. Since the universe and everything within it, are God's manifested Attributes their existence is relative; God's is absolute.

By knowing itself, the Divine essence knows all things within itself. Nevertheless it distinguishes them from itself as objects of its knowledge. This, however,

[1] R. A. Nicholson's translation in his edition of *Tarjumánu 'l-Ashwáq* (Oriental Translation Fund, New Series, vol. xx, p. 19, vv. 13-15).

does not imply that there is some duality between the known object and the knowing subject. Since the Divine essence is the knower, the known and the knowing, there exists complete unity of the subject, the object and the function that establishes a relationship between them.

(B) CREATION

In conformity with the Qur'ān, Ibn 'Arabī regards the world as undergoing an eternal process of creation. In conformity with the Ash'arites (and the atomists) he regards that process as one of constant annihilation and creation. Annihilation here simply means that since an object changes from moment to moment, it cannot be the same once the change has taken place. Since it has ceased to be its old self, that self no longer exists. In order that it might cease to exist, it must obviously have been annihilated. Otherwise there would be not one object but an infinite number of them.

If God exists, and if everything has its being in Him, it follows that the universe was not created at some moment in the distant past—ever since evolving on its own—but that it manifests constantly the Divine existence of its maker. This means that the universe is in a perpetual state of creation. According to Ibn 'Arabī, God does not create anything. Creation means simply the coming into concrete manifestation of something already existing (in God). While this doctrine is in agreement with that of most Muslim philosophers, it is at complete variance with the views of Al-Ghazālī, who regards every spiritual perception and even sensory experience as something entirely new, created afresh by God from moment to moment, as though out of a vacuum.

Though God may will a thing to be, its existence is

made necessary by the very nature of the laws within the thing itself. Actually, for Ibn 'Arabī, God is the name for those laws.

Of particular interest is Ibn 'Arabī's discussion of the way in which the potential existence of things (inherent within God's essence) becomes actual existence in the phenomenal world. This was, of course, a subject that preoccupied most of the philosophers, and one that we associate with Plato's Ideas or the impact of a form (*eidos*) upon matter, in Aristotle. Ibn 'Arabī divides the Divine essence—or, at least, that aspect of it that manifests itself in tangible phenomena—into Divine Names and Divine Attributes. He views a Divine Name as a 'limited' form of the Divine essence prior to its manifestation. We could paraphrase him by saying that a Divine Name is the creative element that holds within itself the potentiality of a particular phenomenon (that might, or might not, come into tangible existence). In other words, it is the active element within the Divine essence out of which a given phenomenon will emerge.

A Divine Attribute, on the other hand, is a Divine Name manifested in the external world. It is the phenomenal object, though not necessarily a material one. For, in Ibn 'Arabī's doctrine, any human thought or activity, too, has its primary being in the Divine essence in which, before its external manifestation, it forms the apposite Divine Name. Whereas a Divine Attribute, being an exteriorization of the Divine Name, must needs be transient and represent the 'passive' element in the procedure, the Divine essence is, of course, unchangeable, indestructible, and embracing both its (potentially) phenomenal and non-phenomenal aspects. Thus it is more than the Platonic Idea, which denotes only the spiritual reality behind a phenomenon, and which disregards the latter's concrete manifestation.

But then, for Plato, such manifestations were mere shadows. For Ibn 'Arabī, they were particular aspects of Reality.

Ibn 'Arabī, in his effort to make his doctrine all-embracing, characteristically treats the same subject in yet other terms. He speaks of Divine consciousness which embraces all the intelligible forms of the prototypes or *a'yān*, as he calls them, and which, as we shall see later, he identifies with the *Logos*, or the Spirit of Muḥammad. The Divine essence embraces all the potential essences of the prototypes, which would seem to be but another title for the Divine Names. Indeed Ibn 'Arabī calls them also 'latent realities' or *Al-a'cyān al-thābitah.* He defines the essence of each of them as a 'mode' of God, and it is through that essence that God becomes conscious of each one of them.

(c) THE ONE AND THE MANY

It should be possible by now to divine how Ibn 'Arabī solves the problem of the unity of God and the multiplicity within the universe or, to put it differently, how he resolves the supposed duality in the relationship between God and His creatures. Naturally, he admits the existence of multiplicity in the world or, in his own words, of the many, *khalq*. But he does not admit the reality of the many in terms of their substance as opposed to essence. He accepts only one Reality, *Al-Ḥaqq* (the *Ana al-Ḥaqq* of Al-Ḥallāj). As viewed by Itself, that is, as God viewing Himself, or when viewed by ourselves as the essence behind all phenomena, their Reality indeed is but one, and can be nothing but one. It can only be regarded as many when viewed solely as *manifestations* of that essence, i.e. when viewed by ourselves in an intellectual or sensory way (that is, as substance).

Ibn 'Arabī's doctrine is by no means identical with the corresponding doctrine of Plotinus, for whom Reality is the *cause* of everything. (In this Plotinus, would be at one with orthodox Muslim doctrine.) For Ibn 'Arabī, the One is not the cause but the essence of everything. This difference in the two doctrines is fundamental. To be the maker of the thing I produce is one matter; it is quite another matter to be the thing itself or, rather, to share with it my essence. To paint the picture of a child is not identical with giving birth to a child.

It should now be evident that for Ibn 'Arabī multiplicity has no spiritual reality, for it is not due to division within the One. It is due to our own individual points of view. As humans, we can see only fragments of the whole. Moreover, we seldom penetrate beyond their surface. According to Ibn 'Arabī, the mystic alone can perceive God in His unity rather than in His alleged multiplicity. It could be said that, for Ibn 'Arabī, the relationship between God and His creatures is that of an object reflected in countless mirrors. These reflections obviously cannot exist without Him, and, in a way, they are He. At the same time they are obviously not He. They are He when we are aware that the reflected image is but a reflection; they are not He when we forget the object they reflect and accept them as final realities. So it is quite permissiable for Ibn 'Arabī to say both: 'I am He and He is I,' and also 'I am He and not He.' His God is both transcendental and immanent.

(D) THE SOUL

If there is really no duality of God and man, we might ask: why should the mystic be so eager to effect a union with God; why should the devout always seek a bridge that would lead him to God? On the basis of Ibn

'Arabī's doctrine, the very words 'meeting' God, 'unification' with God, and so on, are meaningless. For these words presuppose an original separateness from God. For Ibn 'Arabī, union with God is not an eventual reaching or meeting Him but rather a becoming aware of a relationship that has always existed. What the individual soul does is merely to awaken to the realization of its unity with God.[1] The fact that I am (fortunately, but seldom) aware of my liver or my teeth does not presuppose that in order to achieve that awareness I must go outside of myself in search of either of these. Ibn 'Arabī naturally holds that man never becomes God, as God never becomes man. They are always one, even though we are seldom aware of this fact. Only the true mystic can be aware of it.

What Ibn 'Arabī says about Divine essence being conscious of itself *in toto* and also of individual Names, applies equally to his doctrine of the soul. In common with several philosophers, he accepts the doctrine of a Universal Soul. Where he differs from them is in pointing out that the individual soul within it is not 'part' of it. For how, he asks, can soul—a spiritual entity—be divided into parts? The very word 'part' presupposes quantity. Yet within the realm of spirit everything is quality (essence). The Universal Soul is conscious both of itself as a whole and of each individual soul 'within' it. The latter, forming an individual aspect of the Universal Soul, cannot be conscious of the whole but only of itself. Thus God differs from man only in the sense that a thing differs from its individual aspects.

According to Ibn 'Arabī, man consists of three elements: spirit, soul and body. The three aspects of the soul are the rational, vegetative and animal. The

[1] See text from *Kitāb al-Ajwiba*.

rational soul Ibn ʿArabī seems to identify with spirit or the rational principle in man (and not, as does Aristotle, with intellect). The purpose of the vegetative soul is to seek food and to assimilate it. The animal soul has its seat in the physical heart and is shared by man and animals. It represents their vital principle. Both vegetative and animals souls Ibn ʿArabī regards as part of the body. The rational soul, on the other hand, is independent of the body, even though it uses it as a vehicle. It is 'that perfect and simplest substance which is living and active, the substance whose sole activities are remembering, retaining ideas, comprehending, discriminating, and reflecting'.[1]

Viewed superficially, Ibn ʿArabī's division into spirit and body (rationality and animality) might wear a look of dualism. In actual fact both spirit and body are, for him, facets of the same central Reality, one being its inward, the other its outward, aspect. While he admits that the body, unlike the spirit, is destructible, he nevertheless differs from many Muslim philosophers in according it real being. Indeed, how could the body be without such being in view of the fact that it represents the outward aspect of reality?

(E) KNOWLEDGE

The chief aim of early Muslim philosophers was to acquire intellectual command of truths which during the years immediately following the death of the Prophet were accepted unquestioningly on faith. So long as the Muslim community felt no need for rationalizing Quranic truths, it could dispense with the acquisition of a knowledge built on reason. But gradually the Muslims found themselves compelled to explain

[1] *Risālah fī Maʿnā al-Nafs wa-l-Rūḥ*, Publ. by Asin y Palacios, in the *Acts of the 14th Oriental Congress*, Algiers 1905, p. 153.

Quranic revelation in terms intellectually acceptable. Attacks by Christian antagonists alone made such a task imperative. However, as soon as they began to tackle the problem of rational knowledge, questions concerning the technique through which the mind works forced themselves upon their attention. Does knowlege come direct from God or is it the fruit of man's own efforts? Does it reach the mind directly or are complex processes involved? Is the mind one indivisible entity or does it work through separate channels? These and kindred questions had to be answered. The quest for valid answers enabled the philosophers to probe into problems that had only been touched upon by their Greek masters. Some of the answers they evolved have not been invalidated even by modern psychological research. Al-Kindī, writing a thousand years ago, developed a theory (of four types of 'spirit') that nothing in 20th century psychology could easily refute. Ibn Sīnā put forward a doctrine of the internal faculties of perception that, while not dissimilar from Al-Kindī's, surpassed it in precision and elegance. Even Al-Ghazālī turned his attention to the ways by which the mind acquired knowledge; and Ibn Rushd and many others threw new light on that problem.

Ibn 'Arabī was no exception, and many pages of his major works deal with the problem of knowledge. But, as we should expect, his theories differ in their most important aspects from those of other philosophers, even though they show a resemblance with those of the Ṣūfīs. According to him, the soul is born with innate knowledge, but this is 'forgotten' during its association with the body. Thus any newly acquired knowledge is in reality 'old' knowledge suddenly remembered by the soul. Thinking processes he defines as the relating of concepts (already existing in the soul) to each other.

(As Leonardo da Vinci said: 'To understand is to set up a relationship.') Each concept represents an unchangeable idea. A given relationship between concepts cannot change. Each change means that a completely new relationship has been entered into by the concepts or the ideas they represent. (Here Ibn 'Arabī obviously bases himself on Aristotle's theory of the eternal nature of the *eidos* and its subsequent inability to change, a theory accepted by most Muslim philosophers, though not by Al-Ghazālī.)

Where Ibn 'Arabī differs from other Islamic thinkers is in his views on the innermost nature of knowledge. Man's power to apprehend—the power that they usually describe as spirit—he defines as light, *al nūr*. In man this light takes the form of the rational soul which, in turn, is a 'mode' of Universal Reason, *al-'aql al-kullī*, the Aristotelian Agent Intellect or Neo-platonic *Logos*. How then does the light operate in man?[1]

The first step in the acquisition of ordinary knowledge is a sensory perception. But what is it that enables the senses to perceive an object? According to our philosopher, it is the apprehending Light. That Light forms the essence of the senses. The impressions derived by the senses are instantly transferred to the heart which, in turn, passes them on to the intellect. The intellect, located in the brain, recognizes these impressions for what they are, namely sense perceptions, and then transfers them to the imagination. From there they finally reach the understanding (*mufakkirah*), which analyses and tabulates them. The perceptions that are of the greatest interest to the mind are retained by the faculty closest to the heart (not, however, the physical organ), namely memory. Now all the different channels through which perception is being gathered and or-

[1] See text from the *Futūḥāt*.

ganized function thanks to Light. Both mental faculties and sensory perceptions owe their rational character to that Light, the seat of which Ibn 'Arabī identifies with a non-physical centre which he calls the heart or, sometimes, the inward eye, *al-'ayn al-baṣīrah.* Everything that enables us to apprehend life—in fact our very awareness of living—is this light.

It is not always easy to follow Ibn 'Arabī in his explanations of the light. It would appear, however, that he identifies it with our rational soul. We think and feel, hear and see, form images and memorize, by means of various faculties and senses. In their essence all these are light. In other words, light is the quality (or force) through which apprehension takes place. We might call it the inmost essence of our intelligence or that which, in the phenomenal world, is least separated from the Divine.

Now it is the objects of our apprehension that come into question: the phenomena, relationships, actions and, finally, ideas, which the light enables us to apprehend. What is their essence? Since God is the root of everything that is, He is Light *par excellence.* And so all His creatures, men and beasts, ideas, trees and microbes, are manifestations of Light. It follows, therefore, that both the apprehending intelligence and its objects are (functions of) Light. Equally true are the two opposite formulations: what is not Light cannot apprehend Light; and what is not Light cannot be apprehended by Light. Indeed Ibn 'Arabī points out that if a thing or idea cannot be apprehended by any kind of mind, it has no reality. It is even more obvious that what is not Light—for example, the mind of a complete idiot—cannot apprehend the Light (the truth), whether of objects or ideas.

The most perfect knowledge accessible to man is that

of a mystic, Ibn 'Arabī tells us. In the mystic's case Divine essence is revealed directly to the 'heart' in an immediate vision. Such a vision does not depend upon the intellect, and it can dispense with the complicated processes of apprehension requisite for conceptual knowledge. The mystic's heart sees (or reflects) all the Divine perfections which, otherwise, are scattered in endless multiplicity throughout the universe. In fact only the mystic's heart can perceive Reality itself which is beyond thought.

(F) INANIMATE OBJECTS

So far we have not discussed Ibn 'Arabī's views regarding objects other than man and animal. Since he does not attribute to a stone or a twig the rationality that distinguishes man, they might seem to exist in some substratum untouched by the Divine spirit. Yet Ibn 'Arabī, while denying them the *personal* rationality possessed by man, insists that they manifest *Divine* rationality. This results from their following their own inner laws. And, as we know, all laws originate in God. It will be remembered that, according to Ibn 'Arabī, all phenomena are God's Attributes. In so far as all such Attributes have their being in Divine Names which, in turn, are aspects (or localizations) of the Divine essence, they are all identical in origin, though not in their phenomenal manifestation. Must we then assume that a stone's relationship to God does not differ from that of man to God?

Ibn 'Arabī tells us that man alone can know God perfectly (just as God knows Himself through man who is God's consciousness 'in manifestation' that is, exteriorized or made 'visible'). Even the angels know less of God than does man, for they know Him only in His transcendental nature which has no relation to the phenomenal world. Man alone can know God both in His aspects of the Real and the phenomenal. Why Because, of all God's creatures, man alone is both real and phenomenal, eternal and transient, internal and external. Inanimate objects, on the other hand, can know of God only as much as they know of themselves, that is, of God's particular Name revealed through them. They know God's 'stoniness' or what is stone within God; they know what is water, or metal, or cabbage, in Him. Beyond any of these or similar organisms, they can know nothing of God.

(G) THE THING

Under the influence of Plato and Aristotle, Muslim philosophy was greatly preoccupied with the question of what constitutes a thing, or *shay'*. According to the Mu'tazilah, a thing was a concept that could be known regardless of whether it actually existed or not, existence being only one of its various qualities. Ibn 'Arabī, too, conceives of being as possible apart from things that actually exist. It is only in the phenomenal world that the quality of being must be possessed by an object in order that it may exist.

How then does Ibn 'Arabī define non-being? He divides things that have no being into two categories. To the first belong things that have no existence in any of the planes of pure Being, that is God. These he calls pure non-existent. To his second category belong things which exist in one plane but not in another. He divides them into two sub-categories: things which exist only as intellectual concepts without the possibility of existence in the actual world (like, we might say, the concept of a man with a hundred heads or a fire that is wet); and, second, things which have a possible existence in the actual world without, however, existing in it. (Such a thing would have been, for non-Australians, the black swan in the days before Australia was discovered, or any invention prior to its having been made, e.g. the telephone or the jet plane a hundred years ago.) Ibn ʿArabī points out that while these last two categories of non-being can be objects of our thought, pure non-being can never be; in other words, any concept that our mind cannot possibly conceive is pure non-being. This means that pure non-being is everything that cannot be thought of or put into symbols.

Ibn ʿArabī's views are not dissimilar to those of the Ikhwān al-Ṣafā who held that a concept that cannot be expressed in language is unthinkable. So they called the word the 'body of the thought,' and maintained that thought cannot exist without its verbal body. Ibn ʿArabī would certainly not disagree with this, for he regarded both words and thoughts as Divine Attributes and, thus, as partaking in the Divine essence. However, something for which neither a word nor a thought can be found cannot partake of that essence and thus is pure non-existent.

(H) DREAMS

Only with the advent of Jung's analytical psychology has the world become familiar with the concept of the archetypal dreams, dreams whose sources are to be sought not in the subconscious of the individual but in that of an entire civilization or nation. Most people consider the notion of the archetypal dream as not only new but revolutionary. In actual fact it is not new. For Jung's formulation of such a dream can be found in Ibn ʿArabī.

Ibn ʿArabī regards dreams as *khayāl,* or mental images (imaginings) which represent something between the real and the phenomenal worlds, as do our imaginings. He also interprets *khayāl* as anything that provides a symbol for either reality or for some hidden meaning. In this particular sense, the entire phenomenal world might be considered *khayāl*. In fact both that world and dreams he regards as symbols of hidden realities.

It is during dreams that imagination is at its most active, producing ordinary dreams. According to Ibn ʻArabī, it is then that imagination gets hold of experiences of daily life, and presents them to the 'inward eye' (of the heart). In the inward eye, they are magnified as though in a mirror, and it is the subsequently distorted image of those experiences that fill our dreams. Usually these images become the foci or symbols of our desires.

There also exists a second type of dream, which Ibn ʻArabī regards as of far greater significance, the material for which comes not from our ordinary daytime experiences but direct from the Universal Soul, or, as Ibn ʻArabī sometimes calls it, the 'Guarded Table'. In such a dream man's (rational) soul perceives the archetypal ideas contained in the Universal Soul. But even in such dreams imagination gains possession of the received ideas, and distorts them. As a result, man's 'inward eye', while in direct contact with the Universal Soul, nevertheless does not act as a perfect mirror but as a 'running, yet undefiled, stream wherein are reflected illuminated objects of all descriptions'.[1] Thus the dreamer sees only the reflections of the archetypal ideas, and these are merely the symbols of the latter. The symbols have been provided by the dreamer's own imagination and not by the Universal Soul that presented the ideas in all their purity. In consequence, these dreams, being symbolical, have to be interpreted.

[1] From *Māhiyat al-Qalb*, quoted by Affifi, op. cit. p. 132.

For only the reality behind the symbols is real 'knowledge'. (This notion, we might add, would offer opportunities to a Jungian analyst.)

There is, however, one type of dream that is not symbolical but a direct revelation of Reality. Imagination does not enter into it, and the 'inward eye' reproduces the exact reflection of the impression received. In such a dream, the Universal Soul (with its archetypal ideas) reveals itself direct to man's soul without any distortion. (What Ibn 'Arabī means, of course, is that the Universal Soul reveals itself through the medium of the individual soul.) Dreams of this nature obviously call for no interpretation. They are the truly archetypal dreams, and are similar to the mystic's revelation (*waḥy*) or inspiration (*ilhām*). They are the direct vision of Reality, of Universal Truth.

(1) CAUSE AND EFFECT

The hardest test for a non-dualistic philosophy is provided by such distinctly dualistic concepts as those of active and passive, cause and effect, and, finally, good and evil. Aristotelian logic is compelled (by its very nature) to accept the dualistic nature of these concepts. But the acceptance of such a dualism by Ibn 'Arabī would inevitably bring down the entire house of his monistic doctrine. That his doctrine actually passes the test is not due to the author's piecemeal justification, but to the fact that its validity follows organically from the basic principles of his philosophy.

For Ibn 'Arabī's universe is not the effect of a cause that is God, just as a phenomenon is not the Aristotelian outcome of the imprint of form upon matter or, in other words, of the necessary upon the possible. His universe is the outward expression of God's aspects of eternity and infinity. Thus his universe—both the phenomenal, and the invisible that we enter in the hereafter—is a constant process of creation.

In a system in which God provides both (what in Aristotelian terminology must be called) cause and effect, there must exist a like unity of origin on the plane of visible phenomena, and terms such as cause and effect can have no meaning. For Ibn 'Arabī God is the only source of both the lightning and of the destruction produced by it, of both the painter and the painter's picture. Both have their origin in Him, and so God is immanent in both of those phenomena we call cause and effect.

Ibn 'Arabī might have felt justified in explaining away the duality of active and passive by merely identifying the former with cause and the latter with effect. But to seek refuge in intellectual shortcuts was not his way of building up a philosophical system.

In the more conventional systems man appears as the passive agent created by the will of an active God. For Ibn 'Arabī man is passive only when he considers himself as apart from God, that is, exclusively as a phenomenon. As soon, however, as he becomes aware of his God-ness, he is bound to be active. Yet even in that condition he is also passive in so far as his 'active' nature comes from God whose agent he is. Thus he is both active and passive: active when viewed as Divine, passive when viewed as merely phenomenal. However, in Ibn 'Arabī's system these definitions have no real meaning. They represent merely our own mental conceptions born of our tendency to view everything in terms of opposites, contrasts, duality. Duality presupposes the existence of space, a dimension non-existent in pure spirit. It also presupposes the possibility of disharmony or disunity, and opens doors to the 'possible', in contradistinction to the 'necessary'.

Within the realm of pure spirit neither of these can occur. There can only be unity, harmony and necessity. So opposites, with their inevitable concomitants of space, disunity, impermanence, and so on, can be conceived only mentally, when we view the world non-spiritually.

What is true of cause and effect applies equally to active and passive. Thus the object of an action—its 'passive' recipient—is in turn active by his reaction to it. If I hit someone, the reactions of the latter's muscles, nerves, blood vessels, as well as of his mind and emotions, constitute quite as much an 'action' as did the original blow.

(J) GOOD AND EVIL

It is by no means exceptional for Ibn 'Arabī to put forward more than one theory on a given subject, one either amplifying the other or treating it from a different aspect. As we would expect, Ibn 'Arabī's conception of absolute Reality (*Al-Ḥaqq*), which is that of absolute Good (*Al-Khayr al-Maḥḍ*), leaves no room for the duality of good and evil. In the universe, as known to us, he regards evil as non-existence, or rather, as the absence of real existence. Such existence (belonging, as it does, to Reality) must, of course, be 'positive'. Evil is thus the lack of a corresponding positive quality. Darkness is the absence of light, weakness the absence of strength, a lie the absence of truth, illness the absence of health. An organ becomes ill when health has been withdrawn from it. It cannot exist in a condition of 'neutrality'—neither healthy nor unhealthy—illness thus being not a 'quality' negative *per se*, but rather non-health. Everything that *really* exists is for Ibn 'Arabī good—otherwise it could not be there. Consequently he regards evil as a subjective, and not an objective, reality.

In the eyes of God all things must be good. Only man's ignorance calls some of them good and some bad. In his blindness man does not perceive that in the bad things goodness might possibly lie hidden behind their evil appearance. We might cite as an illustration of that truth the positive qualitites of electricity which have always existed in, but which were discovered only after the evil forces inherent in lightning. Before their discovery man could see no good whatsoever therein. Likewise, the positive qualitites within penicillin had potentially always existed within the mildew; but only the mould's negative qualities were known before Alexander Fleming's discovery. In its internal aspect, Ibn ʿArabī considers everything to be good; only in its external aspect, that is as mere appearance (*khalq*) may a thing appear evil.

Since good cannot produce anything that is evil *qua* evil, its evilness derives its apparent reality (that is, in the world of appearance) from man's individual reaction to it. A thing is considered evil because the prevailing convention, morality or religious codes label it as such. It appears as evil because it creates conflicts with certain mental or emotional desires, or because it disagrees with our individual temperament. Ibn ʿArabī insists that even such evil manifestations as lying, disorder, ugliness, sinful action, merely denote the absence of a positive quality, the presence of which would deprive them of their evilness.

Now let us examine Ibn ʿArabī's second interpretation of evil. God's universe would not be perfect if it did not also include imperfections. Perfection, which implies completeness, must include everything, just as a perfect, i.e. complete, colour scheme cannot be limited to 'pretty' colours but must contain every imaginable hue—even 'dirty' greys and browns and black. Without them the scheme would not be complete. It follows from this that, in order to show perfection, the sum-total of happenings and actions within the universe must of necessity include 'imperfect', that is, 'evil', happenings and actions. Since, however, all those actions derive their being from God, it is He who ultimately decrees or commands them.

What then is the meaning of sin, *ma'ṣiyah*, in Ibn 'Arabī's system? According to him, God decrees that an action must take place, but forbids man to perform it or, as he puts it, 'the prophets are asked to communicate God's commandments to the people, but God does not always will that such commandments be fulfilled'. The contradiction implied in this statement is apparent rather than real. What Ibn 'Arabī means is that God decrees an action irrespective of whether, in human eyes, it appears good or evil. God's decree (*al-mashī'ah*) makes such an action as indispensable as it makes the advent of night after day, of autumn after summer, and so on. God does not particularly command the darkness of the night or winter's cold, just as He does not particularly command the evil of any particular action. What He decrees is the action in its totality, irrespective of whether we regard it as good or bad. It is not the evil aspect in the action that He decrees but the action as a whole and as an inevitable expression of His law. In other words. He wills the *action* but not the evil within it. He must approve of *all* actions because they are all His. The conflict (*nizā'*) between them (in so far as they contain what appears to us as evil) and human law or morality exists only for us who are ignorant of the decree behind all God's manifestations. Actions *qua* actions could not become manifest unless they were 'approved' by God.

Sin, then, in Ibn 'Arabī's doctrine, is disobedience

not to God's will (which would be impossible for man), but to the 'mediate religious command'.[1] In God's eyes everything that is must be. Since it must be, it would be futile to define it as either good or evil. All that can be said about it is that it *is*. We are thus entitled to conclude that for Ibn 'Arabī morality, in a spiritual sense, does not exist, or to put it differently, that he considers morality as a purely human code. Within a non-dualistic system such as his, in which everything derives from God, there can be no room for the ordinary concept of morality.

And yet morality enters Ibn 'Arabī's doctrine as it were through a back door. But it is a morality conceived not in the conventional way of relative values—more good or less good, and thus quantitative—but a 'morality' that is purely qualitative, and that derives its validity from purely spiritual considerations. Even in Ibn 'Arabī's scheme man must strive for the good. Yet he must do so, not because such striving denotes virtue or moral soundness, but because it concerns itself with the positive alone. For only the positive—light, truth, health—represent reality, existence. A life of 'evil' is a life of their opposites or 'absences', and thus of spiritual non-existence. It is not an affirmation of life but of escape from it, of only apparent existence.

'Aware' of the dilemma confronting man living in a universe in which everything is willed by Him, God has given man means by which to differentiate between a life of affirmation and one of escapes. It is due to God that man can distinguish between perfection and imperfection, good and evil, harmony and disharmony. If man were not under the obligation to choose the real rather than its opposite and thus the 'moral' rather than the 'immoral', there would be no meaning in God's

[1] *Fuṣūṣ*, p. 319.

injunctions to man to be 'good'. If everything on the *human* level were equally 'good', there would be no validity in some of the Divine Names which, by themselves, imply the 'moral' character of the relationship between God and man. God the Pardoner (*Al-Ghaffār*), the Merciful (*Al-Raḥīm*), the Tormentor (*Al-Mu'adh-dhib*), the Guiding (*Al-Hādī*), would be meaningless if man regarded every one of God's manifestations as equally 'good' (in human terms) and had no need of His mercy or his guidance. In the purely spiritual sphere, that of absolute existence, Ibn 'Arabī obviously cannot accept the dichotomy of good and evil and with it morality. But in the world of appearance, the one in which man normally lives, even he must stress the contrast between moral and the immoral action. However, the decisive factor for him is not the moral aspect of an action but its reality.

(K) FREE WILL AND PREDESTINATION

The problem of free will and predestination preoccupied the Muslim philosophers from the very dawn of their contemplations. The Qur'ān abounds in sayings stressing both man's freedom of action and God's absolute power over man's destiny. The various philosophical schools employed the most ingenious methods to resolve the implicit conflict; but it cannot be said that they ever succeeded in their attempts. The Determinists (*Al-Jabriyyah*) held that man's actions are determined by an outside agent, namely God; according to the Ash'arites, God created man and all his actions; the Mu'tazilah held that while a man's action derives from his free will, his ability to act is God-given. But however subtle their arguments, none of the schools provided a satisfactory reconciliation of the Quranic theses insisting on both God's omnipotence and man's free will.

Ibn 'Arabī disagrees with the doctrine of *jabr* as a compulsion forced upon man from an outside agent. Yet it was obviously impossible for him to accept free will, for this would have left him no alternative but the opposition of man's will to that of God, and thereby have introduced dualism. Since, according to him, everything has its origin and being in God, free will, as ordinarily understood, can have no place in his system. Does it follow that his God as a kind of tyrant who steps in every time man performs an action and imposes His dictate upon him? Does it mean that human choice is governed by a relentless determinism and that man is the helpless victim of Divine arbitrariness? For Ibn 'Arabī man's choice is not dictated by perpetual interference on the part of God but by man's own inner laws. Every leaf, flower and fruit is 'predetermined' already by the seed from which it evolved. It is not Divine capriciousness that makes one seed grow into a big oak tree and another into a weakly maple; their respective inner laws are contained in their seed. Ibn 'Arabī accepts man's own choice, but finds it inherent in his own nature. Since, however, that nature derives from God, free will, in the accepted sense, plays no part in our philosopher's doctrine.

To understand his theory of human will it is necessary first to know that what he really means by 'will' is not exactly our habitual meaning. It signifies, rather, desire, *shahwah*. It is not will but desire that makes a man crave the satisfaction of some appetite. Desire, according to Ibn 'Arabī, is concerned with material objects. Will, on the other hand, is a spiritual force whose object is never a material one. Will drives man towards spiritual fulfilment, and, finally, towards the Divine. As such it is free from all pleasant or unpleasant sensations. Even to feel pleasure at the hope of gaining a vision of God is not the outcome of will but of the desire 'for an object'. But, of course, Ibn 'Arabī's 'will' and its gratification are the privilege of a few exceptional beings, such as the saints and mystics.

Though Ibn 'Arabī occasionally tries to place a personal responsibility on human shoulders ('let him praise no one but himself and blame no one but himself,' he writes in the *Fuṣūṣ* p. 160), such efforts carry no ring of conviction, and we suspect that they were a half-hearted sop to the orthodox. In actual fact he denies free will even to God. God merely decrees what He knows must take place in accordance with the laws that have their being in Him. It is impossible for Him to will what does not lie in the nature of the thing itself. This means that human fate is not pre-determined but *self*-determined. Individual fate is simply man's essential character as it exists from eternity in the Divine knowledge. Man receives as much of good as the 'necessity' of his nature demands. It follows that fate is God's decree concerning things. It is conditioned by His knowledge of their essential nature. So whatever fate decrees is decreed by means of the thing itself. Even God cannot give man either more or less of certain qualities than he actually possesses. In other words, even God cannot perform a miracle that would violate the laws that have their being in Him.

When we consider Ibn 'Arabī's doctrine of free will together with his statements on the nature of good and evil, we find that he is far from being a predeterminist. Though everything is determined by the inner laws governing the nature of the particular agent, it does not follow that the agent is cognisant of those laws. He has to act in almost complete ignorance of them: in other words, he acts as though the 'predetermined' character of his 'choice' were absent. At the same time, if he wishes to lead a life of Reality, he will strive for the positive or that which has true being. Thus, however much the nature of his choice and the outcome of his actions might be determined by his inner laws, he will act as though he were a free agent, and he will even act 'morally', however little conventional morality may be his incentive.

(L) AL-FANĀ'

Ibn 'Arabī devotes a great deal of thought to mystical experiences and the the 'mechanism' within them. The usual Ṣūfī term for 'union' with God is *fanā'* (passing away, or annihilation). But not all Ṣūfīs agree on its meaning, nor on the meaning of its opposite pole, the term *baqā'*, or enduring. Most of the Ṣūfīs before Ibn 'Arabī use the word *fanā'* to describe a purely subjective state. They agree that in *fanā'* consciousness of the phenomenal world is lost; that *fanā'* leads to a gradual unification with God; and that it involves a giving up of all personal desires, and resignation to the will of God. But, as Dr Affifi points out (op. cit., p. 139), with the exception of Al-Qushayrī, no Ṣūfī defines *fanā'* or *baqā'* as clear psychological states: the one as 'abandonment of the phenomenal', the other as 'concentration of the Divine and spiritual'. As Al-Qushayrī says (in his *Risālah*, p. 32), 'the two states together are like a lover's absorption in the beloved'. Practically all other Ṣūfī statements on *fanā'* were vague.

Ibn 'Arabī was not only a Ṣūfī but also a philosopher, whose intellectual capacities were second to none in Muslim thought. In his views on *fanā'* he disagrees not only with most Ṣūfīs but also with those Western mystics who describe a state corresponding to *fanā'*. How can even a mystic, he asks, 'die to self', and yet be conscious of God? Consciousness (irrespective of its object) implies continuation of self. A passing away of self cannot mean anything but sleep. In such a state, 'the mystic is neither with his "self" nor with his "Lord"; he is asleep, he is unaware'. Ibn 'Arabī dismisses as ignorance the assumption that the mystic has become God or died to himself.

Ibn 'Arabī considers *fanā'* from both a mystical and a metaphysical aspect. In a mystical sense, *fanā'* is a passing away of ignorance and a becoming aware of the essential oneness of the whole. It is realization of one's non-existence as form (phenomenon). This, he claims, can be achieved only intuitively. In a metaphysical sense, *fanā'* is a passing away of the forms of the phenomenal world and continuation of the one universal essence. It is the disappearance of form at the moment of the manifestation of God in another form or, as he puts it, 'the disappearance of a form is its *fanā'* at the moment of the manifestation of God in another form'.[1] It can be said then (on the basis of Ibn 'Arabī's, and the atomists', doctrine of the world as being in a constant process of creation, that is, of destruction and recreation) that *fanā'* is catching the infinitesimal moment between the annihilation of one Divine Attribute and the emergence of a new Attribute. (What Ibn 'Arabī appears to mean is that, since Divine Attributes, by their very nature, exist in time, only the 'instant' between them belongs to eternity—the dimension of pure essence. And so it is only then that the timelessness of *fanā'* can be reached.)

In his endeavour to give an objective assessment of *fanā'*, Ibn 'Arabī delineates it as a gradual process which he divides into seven stages. These are as follows:

1. Passing away, from sin. This Ibn 'Arabī does not interpret in the usual Ṣūfī manner as the abandonment

[1] *Fuṣūṣ*, p. 230.

of all sin, but as a realization that all actions are right (not in a moral sense but as coming from God). That which is sin, is to regard one's actions as coming from oneself.

2. Passing away from all actions in the realization that God is the agent of all actions.

3. Passing away from all attributes of the 'form' in the realization that they all belong to God. As Ibn 'Arabī puts it; 'God sees Himself in you through your own eye and, therefore, He really sees Himself: this is the meaning of the passing away of attributes.'[1]

4. Passing away from one's own personality in the realization of the non-existence of the phenomenal self, and the endurance (*baqā'*) of the eternal substance which is its essence.

5. Passing away from the whole world in the realization of the real aspect which is at the bottom of the phenomenal.

6. Passing away from all that is other than God, even from the act of passing away (*fanā' al-fanā'*). The mystic ceases to be conscious of himself as contemplator, God being both the contemplator and the object of the contemplation. (This is very different from the common Ṣūfī view of the disappearance of consciousness which Ibn 'Arabī defines as mere sleep.)

7. Passing away from all Divine attributes. The universe ceases to be the 'effect of a cause' and becomes a 'Reality in appearance' (*Ḥaqq fī Ẓuhūr*). This seventh stage represents the fullest realization of the oneness of all things, and must be the final aim of all mystical endeavour.

It may be objected that Ibn 'Arabī tries in vain to give an intellectually acceptable explanation of the mystical experience, since such an experience is essentially incommunicable. It must, however, be

[1] *Fuṣūṣ*, p. 198.

conceded that no individual experience that involves quality and not merely quantity is communicable except by approximation. No one has ever been able to convey to others the essence of the feeling of being in love, or of the sensation of plunging headlong into icy water. All communication is effected by symbols, whether verbal, mathematical or of any other nature. Though the symbols used by a mystic differ more profoundly from the experience they symbolize than do most symbols from their respective experience, the difference between the two kinds of symbols is not fundamental. If we wish to communicate a mystical experience, we can do it only by employing symbols similar to those we employ when communicating any kind of qualitative experience. These symbols, being media belonging to a plane different from the plane of the things they symbolize, must needs distort the truth of the experience. It may well be that a mystical experience sweeps through the different stages as tabulated by Ibn 'Arabī as though in a flash, and that his detailed tabulation is too complex and artificial to explain it. It may seem too particularized and intellectual, but it contributes to a clearer understanding of the mystical experience.

Summing up, we might say that for Ibn 'Arabī the goal of *fanā'* is the attainment of *true* knowledge by the passing away of everything phenomenal, that is, everything other than God. Attainment of such knowledge can be equated with awareness of God. This, however, must not be interpreted as becoming God. Rather is it God's recognizing Himself through, and within the medium of man.

(M) THE LOGOS

No other Muslim thinker has dealt more thoroughly

with the doctrine of the *Logos* than has Ibn ʿArabī. The Logos doctrine—not necessarily always under that name—plays an important part in Islamic philosophy. In their preoccupation with it Muslim thinkers based themselves inevitably on Plotinus. To some extent Ibn ʿArabī did likewise. Yet, in his hands, that doctrine assumes its own peculiar character. Incidentally, it forms one of the main subjects of his *Fuṣūṣ*.

For Ibn ʿArabī the *Logos* is the creative, animating and rational principle and, as such, Reality of Realities. It is the inward aspect of the Godhead and the Godhead is its outward aspect. It is God's consciousness and, as such, contains all the ideas of existing (or potential) objects, without, however, in itself, having multiplicity. It is through the *Logos* that the world is brought into manifestation. Since the world manifests its perfection, it, too, must be, and indeed is, perfect. Besides being the principle of Divine creativeness, the *Logos* naturally has rationality. In fact it is through the *Logos* that God becomes conscious of Himself. For even in the case of God, thought is a function not of the thinker as a whole but of His mind.

Now, according to Ibn ʿArabī, the Divine consciousness reaches its supreme point in the Perfect Man. So it is in the Perfect man that God knows Himself perfectly. It is to Him that God says (according to a ḥadīth): 'I have not created a creature dearer to me than thee. With thee I give and with thee I take, and with thee I punish.' Evidently Ibn ʿArabī's *Logos* represents the 'agent' through whom God can emerge from His absoluteness, His unknowableness (and, in a sense, unknowingness) into manifestation.

So far Ibn ʿArabī's doctrine would seem to differ but little from that of either Philo or Plotinus. Where he completely parts company with his Greek predecessors is in his interpretation of the manifested *Logos*. Who is this Perfect Man, for him? It is the Prophet Muḥammad. Does this mean that Ibn 'Arabī takes over the Christian doctrine of Incarnation, and assigns to Muḥammad the status of Jesus in Christian dogma? Such a deification of Muḥammad would, of course, be regarded in Islam as polytheism. However unorthodox Ibn 'Arabī might be, he was not likely to propound a doctrine that would have cleared the way for what Muslims consider to be an essential dualism (if not worse) in Christianity. But then his Logos-Muḥammad is not the man Muḥammad from Mecca but Muḥammad as the active principle of Divine knowledge, as the spiritual (and not phenomenal) head of the hierarchy of sainthood and prophethood.

Seeds of a *Logos* doctrine were sown in the Qur'ān itself. In a number of instances the term *rūḥ* (spirit) and *kalimah* (word) are employed to denote a *Logos* concept, as e.g. in Surah iv, 169: 'Verily the Messiah, Jesus the son of Mary, is but the Apostle of God, and His Word which He cast into Mary and a spirit from Him.' On another occasion, Jesus is described as God's word: 'The Messiah, Jesus son of Mary, was only the messenger of God, and His word that He committed to Mary.' In his *Fuṣūṣ*, Ibn 'Arabī calls every prophet a *logos* but not *the Logos*. Saints and prophets are, in his view, the perfect instruments of the universal *Logos*. But while they individually manifest this or that particular aspect of the *Logos*, Muḥammad alone unites in himself all these aspects.

Particularly interesting is our philosopher's interpretation of the difference between the *Logos* (Muḥammad) and mankind to which Adam—another aspect of the *Logos*—stands in a somewhat similar relation to that existing between Muḥammad and other saints. In fact

Muḥammad and Adam are for Ibn 'Arabī practically identical. But while in the phenomenal world Muḥammad is the inward aspect of Adam (Humanity), in the world to come, that is the spiritual, Adam will be the inward aspect and Muḥammad the outward of the same Reality, i.e. the *Logos*.

Now it must be repeated that Ibn 'Arabī does not identify the *Logos* with the earthly person of the Prophet but with the Spirit of Muḥammad, of which the man from Mecca and all the prophets, including Moses, Abraham and Jesus, were individual manifestations. (Though by no means indentical, that relationship is somewhat similar to that between Jesus of Nazareth and Jesus Christ as the incarnation of God the Father.) The entity Muḥammad, combining in itself both the Spirit of Muḥammad and Muḥammad the man, is for Ibn 'Arabī the link between the eternal and the temporal, the Real and the phenomenal. While Muḥammad the man was born, was active, and died in time, the Spirit of Muḥammad exists in all eternity. It is identical with the First Intellect (*Ḥaqīqat al-Ḥaqā'iq*). It is the 'depositor' (*mulqī*) of the *logoi* (*kalimāt*) of the entire world, and, as such, identical with the Holy Spirit (*Rūḥ*). Muḥammad is, thus, the Perfect Man and, as such, the most perfect manifestation of God who Himself is Absolute Perfection.

While every human being is potentially a microcosm, only the Perfect Man is an *actual* microcosm which manifests *all* Divine perfections. Only in him are united all that is manifestable and all the manifestations that, otherwise, exist only separately, whether in a spiritual or phenomenal state. Though Ibn 'Arabī does not actually say so, he almost leaves us under the impression that the Perfect Man (as realized in Muḥammad) surpasses the Godhead in perfection, for he alone is not merely spiritual perfection but equally its phenomenal manifestation. But such an impression would be wrong, for it would suggest (if only by implication) some sort of duality between Godhead and the Perfect Man. Indeed Ibn 'Arabī stresses that the Perfect Man is 'to God as the eye-pupil is to the eye . . . and through him God beholds His creatures'.[1]

While there are many similarities between Ibn 'Arabī's *Logos* doctrine and corresponding doctrines in Christianity, it would be wrong to deduce that the former derives from the latter. Christian *Logos* conceptions are based on the idea of the Incarnation which Ibn 'Arabī utterly rejects. His Spirit of Muḥammad is not a second Person in the Godhead: it is God Himself viewed from a particular aspect. Furthermore, the God of Christianity *is* spirit, *is* love, while Ibn 'Arabī's God is beyond all attributes[2] and acts and reveals Himself only through a particular Agent whom he calls the Spirit of Muḥammad. The difference is far more than merely a semantic one. Paradoxically, it might be said that while the God of Christianity *is* everything and yet becomes Incarnate (in the person of Christ), Ibn 'Arabī's God, while nothing but pure essence that acts through an 'agent', does not require an incarnation. While the God of both Christianity and Islam *created* the universe and is the Creator, Ibn 'Arabī's God manifests Himself in the infinite forms of the universe.

It might be asked why Ibn 'Arabī should have spent so much time and effort upon evolving so complex a doctrine of the *Logos*? We can only assume that, like so many philosophers before him, he found it impossible to conceive of creation, that is, the relationship between

[1] *Fuṣūṣ*, p. 19.

[2] The word 'attribute' is used here in its common sense and not in the specific sense in which Ibn 'Arabī uses it when he refers to Divine Names becoming Divine Attributes.

God and the universe, without some 'hierarchical' system. Hierarchy is inherent in every ordered system. It must needs dominate the macrocosm as well as the microcosm. No man could function properly without organizing his various functions in some inner heirarchy. Thus he will not put the whole of his physical energy into picking up a pin, just as he will not expend the whole of his emotions for a minor pleasure or a minor irritation. An innate hierarchical system within him instinctively makes him assign certain duties to certain inner 'agents' rather than employ the whole of himself for each one of them. Likewise, God does not act (or manifest Himself) *in toto* in the greatest as well as the least significant of His manifestations. He will assign specific agents for specific functions. Hence the acceptance in most religions of archangels, angels, spirits, and so on.

A hierarchical system is of course the basis of most Muslim doctrines of creation as it was of those of the Neo-platonists. But whereas their system implies duality (God on the one hand, and His emanations (or creatures), with the succession of Universal Reason, Spirits of Spheres, the phenomenal world, and so on, on the other), Ibn 'Arabī's system shows no such duality. It might be said that while their heirarchy is a vertical one, beginning with God at the top and reaching matter at the bottom, Ibn 'Arabī's system is a centrifugal one or, rather, one in which all the hierarchies remain within the circle. They are merely the different modes, the inner and outer manifestation of one Reality. That Reality might be said both to act from a centre and to be all-embracing. The doctrines of the philosophers only pretended to solve the problem of duality between a unitarian God and a universe of multiplicity and imperfections, and they did it by the use of such terms as 'emanation' instead of 'creation', 'necessity' of God's nature instead of God's 'will', and so forth. Al-Ghazālī *appears* to have solved the problem by accepting the simpler Quranic doctrine of creation. In actual fact he left the intellectual solution in the air. Ibn 'Arabī would seem to be the only one who solved the problem both from the mystical and the philosophical points of view; that is, in so far as such a problem can ever be solved intellectually, and the solution be expressed through the imperfect medium of language.

We might perhaps summarize Ibn 'Arabī's *Logos* doctrine in the following manner:

Logos is Reality of Realities, first Manifestation of the Absolute; *Logos* is Reality of Muḥammad, not the man of Mecca, but Muḥammad the principle or the Spirit of Muḥammad; the *Logos-Muḥammad* unites in himself all the prophets who, in turn, are minor logoi; the *Logos-Muḥammad* had been manifesting himself in all the genuine prophets long before Muḥammad of Mecca was born.

Each individual prophet manifests but one particular 'Name' of God, whereas the *Logos-Muḥammad*, the Seal of the Prophets, manifests *all* His names; the *Logos-Muḥammad* is the step from the Godhead to the phenomenal universe; it is the link between the eternal and the phenomenal.

And since Ibn 'Arabī approaches the *Logos* problem from more aspects than one, we might conclude by saying that: in its metaphysical aspect the *Logos* is Reality of Realities; in its mystical aspect the *Logos* is Reality of Muḥammad; in its human aspect the *Logos* is the Perfect Man. Naturally all the three are identical, as a man remains the same, irrespective of whether we consider him as a spiritual, biological, intellectual, racial, social or any other entity.

(N) HEAVEN AND HELL

Divine mercy and divine punishment run like a thread through the Qur'ān, and thus heaven and hell play an important part in Muslim doctrine. Whatever else the Qur'ān might be, it most certainly is a book of the most pervasive moral implications. By no stretch of the imagination can the same be said of Ibn 'Arabī's doctrine. In a scheme such as his, there is little room for orthodox morality. In view of this, it is surprising to find that he speaks of both heaven and hell and of the ultimate effects of moral and immoral actions.

Unlike some of the Ṣūfīs, especially Al-Muḥāsibī and Al-Ghazālī, Ibn 'Arabī does not attempt to tell us what we ought to do; how to behave in order to avoid hell and to deserve heaven. Now morality, it has been argued earlier, is primarily a matter of degree and thus of quantity. Ibn 'Arabī is seldom concerned with quantity, with the substantial aspects of the universe. His concern must needs be the essence, the true reality of, and behind, phenomena. And essence, unlike substance, is not a matter of quantity but of quality. Yet since heaven and hell depend upon human behaviour in a moral, that is primarily a quantitative, sense, it would be difficult to equate them with the domain of pure essence.

In spite of all this, Ibn 'Arabī not only speaks of heaven and hell, but he does so in the detailed and luxuriant vocabulary of orthodox Islamic literature, especially of the Ismā'ilians and Carmathians. But, as is to be expected, when he speaks of heaven he means something very different from the orthodox heaven, and his hell has not much in common with the hell of the learned 'ulamā'. While the language he employs in describing these two religions is designed to mollify the orthodox, the meaning behind it is his own. It is in fact the geography of heaven and hell—he even provides a diagram of both these areas—that left so deep a mark upon Dante, and was taken over by him in the *Divine Comedy*.[1] But, having almost overwhelmed us with traditional descriptions of Paradiso and Inferno, Ibn 'Arabī assures us that these are mere words, and he invites us to interpret them as we like or, rather, as he likes.

Inevitably the agonies of hell are for Ibn 'Arabī nothing but symbols, and the existence of both heaven and hell in their conventional meaning is denied by him. He regards both as purely subjective states of the soul. His hell is nothing but the realization by the self of its own enslavement, which is selfhood. One Arabic word for hell, *jahannam*, he interprets as distance, or being-away from God. In consequence, to be in hell means to imagine that a real gulf exists between man and God, and to be oblivious of the fact of their oneness.

Jannah, the Arabic word for heaven, or paradise, he interprets as deriving from *janna*, to conceal. *Jannah* is thus for him the Divine essence in which all multiplicity is concealed; consequently, the realization of absolute unity. In the one case the soul, being the slave of a self that stands between it and the Divine, imagines itself to live in separation from God in a world of multiplicity. In the other case it enjoys the delights of 'living' in a state of complete unity. Since Ibn 'Arabī insists upon the ultimate salvation of every soul, there is in the last analysis really little difference between his heaven and his hell. The only difference between the damned—whose existence he seems to accept merely to be on the safe side with the orthodox—and the blessed is that while the latter will behold the beatific vision, for the former that vision will be too veiled to be

[1] See *Islam and the Divine Comedy*, by Asin y Palacios.

recognized. But, finally, the veils will be removed even from their eyes, and even they will share that experience.

Ibn 'Arabī's heaven and hell appear to have much in common with those of Ibn Sīnā. Yet he is more charitable than the great Persian doctor. It would, however, be wrong to attribute his attitude to sentimentality or to some whim on his part. His heaven and hell form a logical part of a doctrine which cannot possibly admit duality even in after-life. But this essential non-duality of heaven and hell is not 'manufactured' artificially. It forms a logical part of it. How could there be the opposites of 'real' hell and 'real' heaven in a system in which all things, both good and evil, have their being in God or, rather, in their own laws which, however, derive from God? Had Ibn 'Arabī tried to conform to orthodoxy and accepted the traditional heaven and hell, then indeed the unity of his doctrine would have disintegrated into dualism.

(O) LOVE AND BEAUTY

In the Qur'ān, it is the quality of Divine mercy rather than of Divine love that predominates. Love implies reciprocity, and it would be presumptuous of man to assume that his love of God must impel his Maker to love him in return. In Ṣūfī doctrines, of course, love of man and God can be said to form the central core. Ibn 'Arabī is no exception to that rule. But his interpretation of the man-God love relationship differs from that of the other Ṣūfīs. He agrees that the basis of all religions is the worship of God. But could man worship anything without loving the object of his worship? Without love worship is impossible. In fact, for Ibn 'Arabī, love is that which pervades all beings and holds them together. However much love may differ in its forms and expressions, it is fundamentally one, for it represents the

Divine Essence. Since, however, the highest object of man's love is God (or Divine Essence), that object, too, is love. In other words: that which, in man, turns lovingly towards God is, too, of the Divine Essence. As Ibn 'Arabī puts it: 'I swear by the reality of Love that Love is the cause of all love,' and: 'Were it not for Love (residing) in the heart, Love (God) would not be worshipped.'[1] Thus Ibn 'Arabī's inevitable formulation becomes: love loves love. This, of course, is the natural climax of a doctrine of absolute non-dualism. This climax also denotes the dynamic and living quality in the idea and the function of love.

It must follow that for Ibn 'Arabī true worship implies neither the verbal invocation of the Divine name (as by the orthodox in their prayers) nor even the heart's concentration on God (as by the Ṣūfīs). True worship means for him contemplating God lovingly in all His aspects—from the most spiritual to the most material, in short, in everything that exists, including the contemplator himself. This, however, is far from the triumphant and, some would say, vainglorious cry of Al-Ḥallāj, '*Ana al-Ḥaqq*'.

Since the fundamental factor underlying all Divine manifestation is love, we would naturally assume that, for Ibn 'Arabī, love is the supreme purpose of existence: an end than which no other can be of equal worth. And yet he tells us that love as such has no intrinsic value! There is something even beyond love, something that is love's inmost 'cause'. That something is Beauty.

It comes almost as an anticlimax to find a thinker who probes so deeply into the very heart of existence elevating an aesthetic quality—even if it be the highest—to the supreme position in the Divine scheme. Yet even in this unexpected conclusion Ibn 'Arabī is still

[1] *Fuṣūṣ*, pp. 387 & 390, qu. by Affifi, p. 151.

perfectly consistent. For is it not true that love without the incentive of beauty is a mere abstraction? Do we not love only what we consider to be beautiful? The standards of beauty may differ, and that which one person deems beautiful another one may regard as ugly. What matters is that for the lover—even if for no one else—the object of his love must be beautiful. He may be in love with a person regarded by all others as hideous. But if he loves that person, he does so because there is some element of beauty in that person—not necessarily physical—to evoke his love. We may be in love with a reptile or any other creature or object generally regarded as repellent, because even such a creature might well be endowed with beauty visible to us but concealed from others. Rembrandt falls in love with ugly old Jews in Amsterdam or with the darkness of shadows, and Utrillo with the peeling plaster on houses of mean Parisian streets on a grey winter evening; because both artists found beauty in such unlikely models. And because they are deeply in love with those hidden aspects of beauty, they succeed in making that beauty manifest to all.

Man loves God, says Ibn ʿArabī, because God is beautiful. (Al-Fārābī discerned God's beauty in the beauty of the order permeating the God-created universe.) Indeed it is inconceivable that we could love God without considering Him beautiful. An 'ugly' god might be feared, but he cannot be loved. We might offer him our sacrifices, but never our love. God, on the other hand, loves His creatures—man and all creation—because these, too, are beautiful. Whence do they derive beauty? Clearly, it is God's beauty that is the source of every kind of beauty, whether spiritual, intellectual or physical, even though God's own beauty as such must of necessity be beyond all form.

There still remains the question: why should God love the visible beauty as contained in the 'visible' forms of the universe? Ibn 'Arabī tells us that God loves it because in the beauty of created forms His own 'form-less' beauty, in fact His very being, is reflected. 'Does God not say,' Ibn 'Arabī exclaims, 'O David, My yearning for them is greater than their yearning for me?'[1] The 17th century English author, James Howell, seems to have perceived a similar truth when, in his book *Instructions for Forreine Travell* (1642), he wrote: 'By looking downward one can see the stars in the water, but he who looks only upward cannot see the water in the stars.' Without the water the stars could not contemplate their own beauty.

Beauty and the love it inspires are thus the cause of all creation. They are equally the cause of the return of all creatures to God in the double movement of their urge for Him and His urge for them.

[1] *Fuṣūṣ*.

FIVE

IBN 'ARABĪ'S TEXTS

ONE of the main obstacles facing the English-speaking student of Ibn 'Arabī's ideas is the scarcity of translations. The pioneer in this field was Professor R. A. Nicholson of Cambridge who, to the present day, remains the chief exponent of Ibn 'Arabī in the English-speaking world. Though he spared neither time nor ingenuity on this task, even he admitted finding himself often on the brink of defeat. For he found that rendering Ibn 'Arabī into a Western language was a labour almost beyond the capacities of any scholar. 'The vast bulk of Ibnu 'l-'Arabī's writings,' he declared, 'his technical and scholastic terminology, his recondite modes of thought, and the lack of method in exposition have, until recently, deterred European Orientalists from bestowing on him the attention which he deserves.'[1] On another occasion Nicholson declared that 'the theories set forth in the *Fuṣūṣ* are difficult to understand and even more difficult to explain'. In spite of these difficulties he persevered, and it is due mainly to him that we have some Ibn 'Arabī texts in English. The bulk of the texts quoted in the following pages is his work.

(A) FUṢŪṢU 'L-ḤIKAM

The following texts are taken from Ibn 'Arabī's *Fuṣūṣu 'l-Ḥikam* (*The Bezels of Divine Wisdom*) in the

[1] Reynold A. Nicholson, *A Literary History of the Arabs*. Cambridge, University Press, 1907.

translation of the late R. A. Nicholson. Compared to the *Futūḥāt al-Makkiyya*, the *Fuṣūṣ* is a very short work, consisting of twenty-seven chapters, each of which bears the name of one of the prophets. In spite of its comparative brevity, it has always been considered as quite as important as the *Futūḥāt*, and has persistently been commented upon by Muslim philosophers and mystics. Unfortunately, it is a very difficult book to understand and R. A. Nicholson admits that the original text is almost beyond an intelligible rendering into English. 'The author's language is so technical, figurative and involved,' he confesses, 'that a literal reproduction would convey very little.' Nevertheless Professor Nicholson perservered, in the hope that 'by collecting and arranging illustrative passages' and by availing himself 'of the commentator's aid' he might be able to 'throw some light on a peculiarly recondite phase of mystical scholasticism'.

The first passage deals with the nature of God (as does, in fact, the *Fuṣūṣ* in general), in its true, or absolute sense, that is, His essence (*ʿaynuhu*, from *ʿayn*, essence or identity). As has already been implied, God's essences (*aʿyan*) are the same both in Him and in His creatures, His creative word (*kun*, 'be') merely actualizing their existence, according to the law inherent within the creatures themselves, that is, within their essence. But only to the mystic is it given to see that God is one and all, and one is all, a typical Ibn ʿArabī formulation which, while baffling at first, becomes quite simple once we accept the non-dualistic nature of his doctrine.

Sublimity (*ʿulūw*) belongs to God alone. The essences (aʿyān) of things are in themselves non-existent, deriving what existence they possess from

God, who is the real substance (*'ayn*) of all that exists. Plurality consists of relations (*nisab*), which are non-existent things. There is really nothing except the Essence, and this is sublime (transcendent) for itself, not in relation to anything, but we predicate of the One Substance a relative sublimity (transcendence) in respect of the modes of being attributed to it: hence we say that God is (*huwa*) and is not (*lā huwa*). Kharrāz,[1] who is a mode of God and one of His tongues, declared that God is not known save by His uniting all opposites in the attribution of them to him (Kharrāz).[2] He is the First, the Last, the Outward, the Inward; He is the substance of what is manifested and the substance of what remains latent at the time of manifestation; none sees Him but Himself, and none is hidden from Him, since He is manifested to Himself and hidden from Himself; and He is the person named Abū Sa'īd al-Kharrāz and all the other names of originated things. The inward says 'No' when the outward says 'I', and the outward says 'No' when the inward says 'I', and so in the case of every contrary, but the speaker is One, and He is substantially identical with the hearer. . . . The Substance is One, although its modes are different. None can be ignorant of this, for every man knows it of himself,[3] and Man is the image of God.

Thus things became confused and numbers appeared, by means of the One, in certain degrees.[4]

[1] Abū Sa'īd al-Kharrāz (ob. A.D. 890) was a well-known Ṣūfī of Baghdad.

[2] The mystic cannot know God unless he is illuminated by all the Divine attributes, so that he becomes a *haqq*.

[3] Every individual is conscious of having different faculties and qualities.

[4] One in the first degree is one, in the second ten, in the third a hundred, in the fourth a thousand, and each of these degrees comprises simple and complex numbers, just as species comprise individuals and genera species.

The One brought number into being, and number analysed the One, and the relation of number was produced by the object of numeration. . . . He that knows this knows that the Creator who is declared to be incomparable (*munazzah*) is the creatures which are compared (*mushabbah*) with Him—by reason of His manifesting Himself in their forms—albeit the creatures have been distinguished from the Creator. The Creator is the creature, and the creature is the Creator: all of this proceeds from One Essence; nay, He is the One Essence and the many (individualized) essences. . . . Who is Nature and Who is all that is manifested from her?[1] We did not see her diminished by that which was manifested from her, or increased by the not-being of aught manifested that was other than she. That which was manifested is not other than she, and she is not identical with what was manifested, because the forms differ in respect of the predication concerning them: this is cold and dry, and this is hot and dry: they are united by dryness but separated by cold and heat. Nay, the Essence is (in reality) Nature. The world of Nature is many forms in One Mirror; nay, One Form in diverse mirrors.[2] Bewilderment arises from the difference of view, but those who perceive the truth of what I have stated are not bewildered.

In the following passages Ibn ʿArabī discusses the nature and function of man in relation to God:

When God willed in respect of His Beautiful

[1] Real Being, when limited by a universal individualization, is Nature, from which are manifested secondary and tertiary individualizations, viz., natural bodies of various kinds.

[2] Nature may be regarded either as all the particular forms in which Reality reveals itself or as the universal form of Reality revealing itself in all particular forms.

Names (attributes), which are beyond enumeration, that their essences (*a'yān*)—or, if you wish you may say 'His essence (*'aynuhu*)'—should be seen, He caused them to be seen in a microcosmic being (*kawn jāmi'*) which, inasmuch as it is endowed with existence,[1] contains the whole object of vision, and through which the inmost consciousness (*sirr*) of God becomes manifested to him. This He did, because the vision that consists in a thing's seeing itself by means of itself is not like its vision of itself in something else that serves as a mirror for it: therefore God appears to Himself in a form given by the place in which He is seen (i.e. the mirror), and He would not appear thus (objectively) without the existence of this place and His epiphany to Himself therein. God had already brought the universe into being with an existence resembling that of a fashioned soulless body, and it was like an unpolished mirror.[2] Now, it belongs to the Divine decree (of creation) that He did not fashion any place but such as must of necessity receive a Divine soul, which God has described as having been breathed into it; and this denotes the acquisition by that fashioned form of capacity to receive the emanation (*fayd*), i.e., the perpetual self-manifestation (*tajallī*) which has never ceased and never shall. It remains to speak of the recipient (of the emanation). The recipient proceeds from naught but His most holy emanation, for the whole affair (of existence) begins and ends with

[1] i.e., relative existence, wherein Absolute Being is reflected.

[2] The world of things was brought into existence before the creation of Man, in so far as every Divine attribute (universal) logically implies the existence of its corresponding particular, which is the Essence individualized by that relation, whereas Man alone is the Essence individualized by all relations together. Since the universe could not manifest the unity of Being until Man appeared in it, it was like an unpolished mirror or a body without a soul.

Him: to Him it shall return, even as from Him it began.[1]

The Divine will (to display His attributes) entailed the polishing of the mirror of the universe. Adam (the human essence) was the very polishing of that mirror and the soul of that form, and the angels are some of the faculties of that form, viz., the form of the universe which the Ṣūfīs in their technical language describe as the Great Man, for the angels in relation to it are as the spiritual and corporeal faculties in the human organism[2]. . . . The aforesaid microcosmic being is named a Man (*insān*) and a Vicegerent (*khalīfa*). He is named a Man on account of the universality of his organism and because he comprises all realities.[3] Moreover, he stands to God as the pupil (*insān*), which is the instrument of vision, to the eye; and for this reason he is named a Man. By means of him God beheld His creatures and had mercy on them.[4] He is Man, the originated (in his body), the eternal (in his spirit); the organism everlasting (in his essence), the Word that divides and unites. The universe was completed by his existence, for he is to the universe what the bezel is to the seal—the bezel whereon is graven the signature

[1] The 'most holy emanation' (*al-fayḍu 'l-aqdas*) is the eternal manifestation of the Essence to itself. This emanation is received by the essences of things (*al-a'yānu 'l-thābita*) in the plane of unity-in-plurality (*wāḥidiyya*), i.e., in the Divine knowledge where no distinctions exist. From one point of view, God is never revealed except to Himself; from another, He is revealed to 'recipient' modes of Himself, to each in accordance with its 'capacity'.

[2] I have omitted a few lines here, to the effect that Man unites all aspects of God—the oneness of the Essence, the plurality of the Divine attributes, and the world of nature. This truth, the author adds, cannot be apprehended save by mystical perception. R.A.N.

[3] i.e., the etymological explanation of the name *insān* is that Man *yu'nis* or *yu'anis* (knows or is familiar with) all things: the three Arabic words are derived from the same root. R.A.N.

[4] By bringing them into existence.

that the King seals on his treasuries.[1] Therefore He named him a Vicegerent, because he guards the creatures (of God) just as the King guards his treasuries by sealing them; and so long as the King's seal remains on them, none dares to open them save by his leave. God made him His Vicegerent in the guardianship of the universe, and it continues to be guarded whilst this PERFECT MAN is there. Dost not thou see that when he shall depart (to the next world) and his seal shall be removed from the treasury of this world, there shall no more remain in it that which God stored therein, but the treasure shall go forth, and every type shall return to its (ideal) antitype, and all existence shall be transferred to the next world and sealed on the treasury of the next world for ever and ever?

This was the knowledge of Seth, and it is his knowledge that replenishes every spirit that discourses on such a theme except the spirit of the Seal (the Perfect Man), to whom replenishment comes from God alone, not from any spirit; nay, his spirit replenishes all other spirits. And though he does not apprehend that of himself during the time of his manifestation in the body, yet in respect of his real nature and rank he knows it all essentially, just as he is ignorant thereof in respect of his being compounded of elements. He is the knowing one and the ignorant, for as the Origin (God) is capable of endowment with contrary attributes—the Majestical, the Beautiful, the Inward, the Outward, the First, the Last—so is he capable thereof, since he is identical (*'ayn*) with God, not

[1] Man's heart (*qalb*) bears the impression of the Greatest Name of God (i.e., the Essence) together with all the other Divine Names.

other than He.[1] Therefore he knows and knows not, perceives and perceives not, beholds and beholds not.[2]

Ibn 'Arabī further illustrates the interdependence of God and man, the latter acting as the eye through which God can see His own creation, in the following verses from the *Fuṣūṣ* in which the words within brackets form the commentary of 'Abdu 'l-Razzāq al-Kāshānī:

'He praises me (by manifesting my perfections and creating me in His form),
And I praise Him (by manifesting His perfections and obeying Him).
How can He be independent when I help and aid Him? (because the Divine attributes derive the possibility of manifestation from their human correlates).
For that cause God brought me into existence.
And I know Him and bring Him into existence (in my knowledge and contemplation of Him).

In the following passage Ibn 'Arabī contrasts the finite God of religion with the infinite God of the mystic or, it might be said, God as beheld by even the most pious worshipper with God in His absoluteness, that is God not limited by any man's experience of Him.

The believer praises the God who is in his form of belief and with whom he has connected himself. He praises none but himself, for his God is made by himself, and to praise the work is to praise the maker

[1] Man is Absolute Being limited by individualization (*ta'ayyun*). This limitation however, is negative and unreal: it consists in failure to receive all individualizations, to be endowed with all attributes, to be named with all names. In so far as Man is a reality (*ḥaqq*) he is not a human creature (*khalq*).

[2] *Fuṣūṣ*, 39 fol.

of it: its excellence or imperfection belongs to its maker. For this reason he blames the beliefs of others, which he would not do, if he were just. Beyond doubt, the worshipper of this particular God shows ignorance when he criticizes others on account of their beliefs. If he understood the saying of Junayd, 'The colour of the water is the colour of the vessel containing it,'[1] he would not interfere with the beliefs of others, but would perceive God in every form and in every belief. He has opinion, not knowledge: therefore God said, 'I am in My servant's opinion of Me,' i.e., 'I do not manifest Myself to him save in the form of his belief.' God is absolute or restricted, as He pleases; and the God of religious belief is subject to limitations, for He is the God who is contained in the heart of His servant. But the absolute God is not contained by anything, for He is the being of all things and the being of Himself, and a thing is not said either to contain itself or not to contain itself.[2]

Our last passage from the *Fuṣūṣ* deals in Ibn 'Arabī's typical scholastic manner with the subject of mercy:

Every one whom Mercy remembers is blessed, and there is nothing that Mercy has not remembered. Mercy's remembrance (*dhikr*) of things is identical with her bringing them into existence:[3] therefore every existent thing is an object of mercy. Do not let thy perception of what I say be hindered by the doctrine of everlasting punishment. Know, first, that

[1] i.e., God is revealed in different forms of belief according to the capacity of the believer. The mystic alone sees that He is One in all forms, for the mystic's heart (*qalb*) is all-receptive: it assumes whatever form God reveals Himself in, as wax takes the impression of the seal (*Fuṣūṣ*, 145).

[2] *Fuṣūṣ*, 282. cf. 135.

[3] cf. p. 98 fol.

Mercy's bringing into existence comprises all, so that the pains of Hell were brought into existence by Mercy. Then, secondly, Mercy has an effect in two ways: (1) an essential effect, which is her bringing into existence every '*ayn* (individual idea) without regard to purpose or absence of purpose, or to what is congruous or incongruous, for she was beholding every '*ayn* as it existed in the knowledge of God before its actual existence, and therefore she saw the reality (*ḥaqq*), created in men's beliefs, as a potentially existent '*ayn*, and showed mercy to it by bringing it into existence (in their beliefs). Accordingly, we have said that the reality created in men's beliefs was the first object of mercy, after mercy was shown by bringing into existence the individual believers. (2) An effect produced by asking (*su'al*): those who are veiled from the truth ask God[1] to have mercy upon them in their belief, but the mystics ask God that Mercy may subsist in them,[2] and they ask for mercy in God's name, saying, 'O God, have mercy upon us!' That which has mercy upon them is the subsistence of Mercy in them.[3]

(B) AL-FUTŪḤĀT AL-MAKKĪYA

Ibn 'Arabī's *al-Futūḥāt al-Makkyīa* (Cairo A.H. 1293) or *The Meccan Revelations* may be said to represent its author's magnum opus. It is an enormous treatise consisting of five hundred and sixty chapters and embodying the core of Ibn 'Arabī's philosophico-mystical doctrine. The author claims that he was com-

[1] i.e., the finite Lord (*rabb*) who stands in a special and different relation to every object of lordship (*marbūb*). cf. *Fuṣūṣ*, 95.

[2] i.e., the true mystic prays that he may be 'illumined' with the Divine attribute of Mercy so as to become a *raḥīm*, which necessarily involves a *marḥūm*, and to know himself as a mode of the absolute God who is in reality both the *raḥīm* and the *marḥūm*.

[3] *Fuṣūṣ*, 225.

manded to write this work on the orders of the Prophet Muḥammad himself whom he beheld seated on a throne amidst angels, prophets and saints. He also claims that, while, on one occasion, circumambulating the Ka'ba at Mecca, he met a youth (symbolizing a celestial spirit) who revealed to him the esoteric Temple hidden to profane eyes, even as divine truth is hidden behind the veils of popular religion. Without penetrating those veils, man cannot perceive God's true nature. The youth commanded Ibn 'Arabī to record the mysteries that he would reveal to him. He led the philosopher into the Ka'ba, and, appearing to him on a three-legged steed, breathed into him the comprehension of all things.

That comprehension, however, came to him only gradually, through a succession of different visions. Some of these were obtained through an ascension to heaven, an ascension that, both in its general plan and in numerous details, we find repeated in Dante's *Divine Comedy*. Ibn 'Arabī's ascension proceeded through seven stages corresponding to the astronomical heavens from the Moon to Saturn. In each of these, he met the various prophets who revealed to him certain sets of mysteries. Thus in the first heaven, that of the Moon, Adam instructed him on the significance of the divine names; on changes in the material elements; on the generation of all living things including man. In the second heaven, that of Mercury, Jesus and John revealed to him secrets about the performance of miracles. In the subsequent heavens, prophets from Joseph and Enoch to Moses and Abraham instructed him in subjects ranging from the astronomical causes of night and day and the interpretation of dreams to the life hereafter. In the second part of the ascension, the author reached the four mystic rivers, representing the Pentateuch, the Book of Psalms, the Gospel and the

Qur'ān. Farther still, he penetrated to the sphere of the Fixed Stars in which dwelt the angelic spirits. After crossing the sphere of the Zodiac, he reached the stool upon which rest the feet of God, symbols of His justice and mercy. Facing the throne of God, he learned the mysteries of the cosmos, and, finally, beheld the utmost secrets of the divine essence.

The visions obtained thanks to the help of the youth met outside the Ka'ba form the contents of the *Futūḥūt*. Ibn 'Arabi claimed that every word of that book reached him by supernatural means.

The following extract from the *Futūḥūt* (iii, p. 365), taken from Margaret Smith's *Readings from the Mystics of Islam* (Luzac & Co., 1950), deals with the subject of human knowledge, or apprehension, or truth which, as will be remembered, has its being in Light (*al-nūr*):

> The veils of darkness and light, by which God is veiled from the world, are only what describes the contingent, because it is in the midst and it looks only to itself and it does not look to what is within the veil. If the veils were raised from the contingent the contingency would be revealed and the necessary and the imaginable, because the veil is raised, but the veils continue to be a concealment, and it must be so. Consider this world in regard to the raising of the veil, for He spoke of consuming, by the glory of His countenance, the creature who apprehends it and sometimes He says of Himself that the creatures can see Him and not be consumed, declaring that the veils are raised in the Vision, and the Vision itself is a veil. 'The eye of His creature does not see Him,' and if men understood the meaning of this, they would know themselves, and if they knew themselves, they would know God: and if they really knew God, they

would be satisfied with Him and would think about Him alone, not about the kingdom of the heavens and the earth. If, indeed, they knew the truth of the matter, they would realize that He is Himself the Essence of the kingdom of the heavens and the earth.

If it were not for the Light, nothing at all could be apprehended by the mind or the senses or the imagination, which we also call by different names. According to the common folk, the name is given to the mind, and among the gnostics, to the light of perception; when you apprehend what is audible, you call the light which apprehends, hearing, and when you apprehend what is visible, you call the light seeing. Light involves a relationship, for apprehending what is apparent. Everyone who perceives must have some relationship to the light, by which he is made able to perceive, and everything which is perceived has a relationship with God, Who is Light, that is, all which perceives and all which is perceived.

In the following passages[1] of the *Futūḥāt* Ibn 'Arabī describes 'the glorious triumph of the elect':

The blessed gather around the snow-white hill to await the epiphany of the Lord. As they stand, each in his respective grade and place and magnificently arrayed, a dazzling light shines forth before which they fall prostrate. Through their eyes into the inmost recesses of their bodies and souls the light penetrates, so that each of the blessed becomes all eye and ear and sees and hears with his entire spirit, such is the virtue conferred on them by the light. Thus are they prepared for the presence of the Almighty.

[1] Quoted in *Islam and the Divine Comedy,* by Miguel Asin, translated by Harold Sunderland. London, John Murray, 1926, pp. 157-9.

And then the Prophet appears before them, saying, 'Prepare, then, ye chosen, for the manifestation of the Lord.' The three veils that enshroud the Almighty—the veils of glory, majesty and power—are drawn aside at His will, and the truth is revealed. . . .

This vision, although in itself one and the same so far as the elect are concerned, has, nevertheless, different aspects. Those prophets, who only acquired their knowledge of God through the faith received from God Himself and did not increase that knowledge by reason and contemplation, will behold the vision through the eye of faith. The saint whose faith in God was inspired by a prophet will see it through the mirror of that prophet. If, however, he also gained a knowledge of God through contemplation, then will he have two visions, one of science and the other of faith. . . . Those who obtained from God the mystic intuition only will occupy a grade in glory apart from all the other elect. To sum up, the three aspects which God presents to the elect in these three categories are graded thus: the prophets who received supernatural inspiration from God excel those saints who followed their teaching; while those who were neither prophets nor their disciples but simply saints and friends of God will, if they achieved the desired end by rational contemplation, be inferior in the Beatific Vision to the mystics, because reason, like a veil, will intervene between them and the Divine truth, and their efforts to raise it will be of no avail. In like manner the followers of the prophets will be unable to raise the veil of prophetic revelation. And so it is that the Beatic Vision, pure and unalloyed, will be the heritage exclusively of the prophets and the mystics who, like the prophets, received Divine inspiration on earth. . . .

In the Beatic Vision God manifests Himself to the elect in a general epiphany, which, nevertheless, assumes various forms corresponding to the mental conceptions of God formed by the faithful on earth. There is, then, one single epiphany, which is multiple only by reason of the difference of forms in which it is received. The Vision impregnates the elect with Divine Light, each experiencing the Vision according to the knowledge of the Divine dogma or dogmas gained by him on earth.

The Divine light pervades the beings of the elect and radiates from them, reflected as if by mirrors, on everything around them. The spiritual enjoyment produced by the contemplation of this reflection is even greater than that of the Vision itself. For, at the moment when they experience the Beatific Vision, the elect are transported and, losing all consciousness, cannot appreciate the joys of the Vision. Delight they feel, but the very intensity of the delight makes it impossible for them to realize it. The reflected light, on the other hand, does not overpower them, and they are thus able to participate in all its joys. . . .

Each knows his allotted grade and seeks it as a child seeks its mother's breast, and iron, the lodestone. To occupy or even aspire to a higher grade is impossible. In the grade in which he is placed each sees the realization of his highest hopes. He loves his own grade passionately and cannot conceive that a higher could exist. If it were not so, heaven would not be heaven but a mansion of grief and bitter disillusion. Nevertheless, those in the superior participate in the enjoyment of the lower grades.

(c) KITĀB AL-AJWIBA

In the following passages from *Kitāb al-Ajwiba*, (in

Margaret Smith's translation[1]) Ibn 'Arabī deals again with the subject of the true nature of God, treated already in our first extract from the *Fuṣūṣ* (see pp. 68–9). This subject of God's One-ness and All-ness is, of course, of fundamental importance to Ibn 'Arabī's entire philosophy, and he returns to it again and again. In the following extract he also emphasizes the closeness, nay the very identity, of phenomenal existence and divine existence, and of God's 'dependence' upon His creatures. He touches here also upon another of his fundamental themes, namely that of the awakened soul's realization that it is 'no other than God'.

He is and there is with Him no before or after, nor above nor below, nor far nor near, nor union nor division, nor how nor where nor place. He is now as He was, He is the One without oneness and the Single without singleness. . . . He is the very existence of the First and the very existence of the Last, and the very existence of the Outward and the very existence of the Inward. So that there is no first nor last nor outward nor inward except Him, without those becoming Him or His becoming them. He is not in a thing nor a thing in Him, whether entering in or proceeding forth. It is necessary that you know Him, after this fashion, not by learning (*'ilm*) nor by intellect, nor by understanding, nor by imagination, nor by sense, nor by the outward eye nor by the inward eye, nor by perception. By Himself He sees Himself and by Himself He knows Himself. . . . His veil, that is, phenomenal existence, is but the concealment of His existence in His oneness, without any attribute. . . . There is no other and there is no existence for any other, than He. . . . He whom you think to be other

[1] op. cit., p. 98.

than God, he is not other than God, but you do not know Him and do not understand that you are seeing Him. He is still Ruler as well as ruled, and Creator as well as created. He is now as He was, as to His creative power and as to His sovereignty, not requiring a creature nor a subject. . . . When He called into being the things that are, He was already endowed with all His attributes and He is as He was then. In His oneness there is no difference between what is recent and what is original: the recent is the result of His manifestation of Himself and the original is the result of His remaining within Himself.

There is no existence save His existence. To this the Prophet pointed when he said: 'Revile not the world, for God is the world,' pointing to the fact that the existence of the world is God's existence without partner or like or equal. It is related that the Prophet declared that God said to Moses: 'O My servant, I was sick and thou didst not visit Me: I asked help of thee and thou didst not give it to Me,' and other like expressions. This means that the existence of the beggar is His existence and the existence of the sick is His existence. Now when this is admitted, it is acknowledged that this existence is His existence and that the existence of all created things, both accidents and substances, is His existence, and when the secret of one atom of the atoms is clear, the secret of all created things, both outward and inward, is clear, and you do not see in this world or the next, anything except God, for the existence of these two Abodes and their name and what they name, all of them are assuredly He.

When the mystery—of realizing that the mystic is one with the Divine—is revealed to you, you will understand that you are no other than God and that you have continued and will continue . . . without when and without times. Then you will see all your actions to be His actions and all your attributes to be His attributes and your essence to be His essence, though you do not hereby become He or He you, in either the greatest or the least degree. 'Everything is perishing save His Face,' that is, there is nothing except His Face, 'then, withersoever you turn, there is the Face of God.'

Just as he who dies the death of the body, loses all his attributes, both those worthy of praise and those worthy of condemnation alike, so in the spiritual death all attributes, both those worthy of praise and those to be condemned, come to an end, and in all the man's states what is Divine comes to take the place of what was mortal. Thus, instead of his own essence, there is the essence of God and in place of his own qualities, there are the attributes of God. He who knows himself sees his whole existence to be the Divine existence, but does not realize that any change has taken place in his own nature or qualities. For when you know yourself, your 'I-ness' vanishes and you know that you and God are one and the same.

(D) THE TARJUMĀN AL-ASHWĀQ

So far as I am aware, the only complete work of Ibn 'Arabī translated into English is the *Tarjumān al-Ashwāq*, which Prof. R. A. Nicholson published in 1911.[1] In his Introduction, the translator explains the

[1] The *Tarjumān Al-Ashwāq*, A Collection of Mystical Odes, by Muyi'ddin Ibn Al-Arabi. Edited from three Manuscripts with a literal version of the text and an abridged translation of the author's commentary thereon by Reynold A. Nicholson, M.A., Litt.D, Lecturer in Persian in the University of Cambridge, and formerly Fellow of Trinity College. Oriental Translation Fund, New Series. Vol. XX London: Royal Asiatic Society, 22 Albemarle Street. 1911.

reasons that prompted him to undertake his task. 'The fact', he says, 'that this book is accompanied by a commentary, in which the author himself explains the meaning of almost every verse, was the principal motive that induced me to study it; its brevity was a strong recommendation. . . .' But he also warns the reader of the book's 'obscurity of style and the strangeness of its imagery'. As its redeeming features he mentions, however, its 'many noble and striking thoughts' and its passages 'of real beauty'.

When Ibn 'Arabī first brought his collection of odes '*Interpreter of Desires*' before his public, these were unaccompanied by any commentary. But the undisguisedly love character, not to say erotic element of the odes shocked many of their readers who apparently failed to recognize their true mystical nature. In consequence, Ibn 'Arabī brought out a new edition of his poems, accompanied by a new preface and by the commentaries that, ever since, have formed an integral part of the volume. His purpose in writing the poems as well as the later commentaries emerges from his Prefaces from which the following quotations are taken:

'Makīnu'ddīn had a young daughter, called Niẓām and surnamed 'Aynu'sh-Shams wa'l-Bahā, who was exceedingly beautiful and was renowned for her asceticism and eloquent preaching. Ibn 'Arabī observed the nobility of her nature, which was enhanced by the society of her father and aunt.' (The latter, Fakhru'n-Nisā bint Rustam, was a lady of very advanced age and great devotion who had shared with Ibn 'Arabī her readings of the Apostolic Traditions.) 'He celebrated her in the poems contained in this volume, using the erotic style and vocabulary, but he could not express even a small part of the feelings roused in him by the recollection of his love for her in past times. . . .'

The author continues: 'Whenever I mention a name in this book I always allude to her, and whenever I mourn over an abode I mean her abode. In these poems I always signify Divine influences and spiritual revelations and sublime analogies, according to the most excellent way which we (Ṣūfīs) follow . . . God forbid that readers of this book and of my other poems should think of aught unbecoming to souls that scorn evil and to lofty spirits that are attached to the things of Heaven! Amen: . . . I have used the erotic style and form of expression because men's souls are enamoured of it, so that there are many reasons why it should commend itself.'

In spite of his warning to the reader of the nature and purpose of his style—a style employed by most Ṣūfī poets—Ibn 'Arabī found himself attacked, and ultimately felt constrained to add commentaries to the poems, commentaries that, in most cases, are much longer than the poems themselves. In a new Preface, he explained the purpose of his commentaries in the following words:

'I wrote this commentary on the *Dīwān* entitled *Tarjumān al-Ashwāq*, which I composed at Mecca, at the request of my friend al-Mas'ūd Abū Muḥammad Badr b. 'Abdallāh al-Ḥabashī al-Khādim and al-Walad al-Barr Shamsu'ddīn Ismā'īl b. Sūdakīn an-Nūrī in the city of Aleppo. He (Shamsu'ddīn) had heard some theologian remark that the author's declaration in the preface to the *Tarjumān* was not true, his declaration, namely, that the love-poems in this collection refer to mystical sciences and realities. 'Probably', said the critic, 'he adopted this device in order to protect himself from the imputation that he, a man famous for religion and piety, composed poetry in the erotic style.' Shamsu'ddīn was offended by his observations and repeated them to me. Accordingly, I began to write the commentary at Aleppo, and a portion of it was read aloud in my lodgings in the presence of the above-mentioned theologian and other divines. . . . I finished it with difficulty and in an imperfect manner, for I was in haste to continue my journey. . . . When my critic heard it he said to Shamsu'ddīn that he would never in future doubt the good faith of any Ṣūfīs who should assert that they attached a mystical signification to the words used in ordinary speech; and he conceived an excellent opinion of me and profited (by my writings). This was the occasion of my explaining the *Tarjumān.*'

For a reader used to the erotic character of so much in Ṣūfī poetry the mystical content of Ibn 'Arabī's odes will reveal itself without undue difficulty. It is quite obvious that Niẓām was for the poet what Beatrice was for Dante, namely an embodiment of divine love and beauty, a symbol and a spiritual ideal. Yet though the reader may instantly sense the mystical nature of the poems, he would hardly seem likely to find the key to their true meaning without Ibn 'Arabī's guidance. In fact the poet admitted that in certain of his odes the mystical meaning was not quite clear even to himself. This is hardly surprising considering the fact that he claimed to have written them in a state of ecstasy. Though it cannot be asserted that the commentaries always clarify the sense of the odes, without them, even the reader accustomed to Ṣūfī terminology might well find himself defeated by the obscurity and complexity of the poems.

PART TWO

A SELECTION FROM TARJUMĀNU AL-ASHWĀQ

I

1. Would that I were aware whether they knew what heart they possessed!
2. And would that my heart knew what mountain-pass they threaded!
3. Dost thou deem them safe or dost thou deem them dead?
4. Lovers lose their way in love and become entangled.

COMMENTARY

1. 'They', i.e. the Divine Ideas of which the hearts (of gnostics) are passionately enamoured, and by which the spirits are distraught, and for whose sake the godly workers perform their works of devotion.

'What heart': he refers to the perfect Muhammadan heart, because it is not limited by stations. Nevertheless, it is possessed by the Divine Ideas, for they seek it and it seeks them. They cannot know that they possess it, for they belong to its essence, inasmuch as it beholds in them nothing except its own nature.

2. 'What mountain-pass they threaded', i.e. what gnostic's heart they entered when they vanished from mine. 'Mountain-pass' signifies a 'station', which is fixed, in contrast to a 'state', which is fleeting.

3. The Divine Ideas, *qua* Ideas, exist only in the existence of the seer; they are 'dead' in so far as the seer is non-existent.

4. Lovers are perplexed between two opposite things,

for the lover wishes to be in accord with the Beloved and also wishes to be united with Him, so that if the Beloved wishes to be separated from the lover, the lover is in a dilemma.

II

1. On the day of parting they did not saddle the full-grown reddish-white camels until they had mounted the peacocks upon them.
2. Peacocks with murderous glances and sovereign power: thou wouldst fancy that each of them was a Bilqis on her throne of pearls.
3. When she walks on the glass pavement thou seest a sun on a celestial sphere in the bosom of Idris.
4. When she kills with her glances, her speech restores to life, as tho' she, in giving life thereby, were Jesus.
5. The smooth surface of her legs is (like) the Tora in brightness, and I follow it and tread in its footsteps as tho' I were Moses.
6. She is a bishopess, one of the daughters of Rome, unadorned: thou seest in her a radiant Goodness.
7. Wild is she, none can make her his friend; she has gotten in her solitary chamber a mausoleum for remembrance.
8. She has baffled everyone who is learned in our religion, every student of the Psalms of David, every Jewish doctor, and every Christian priest.
9. If with a gesture she demands the Gospel, thou wouldst deem us to be priests and patriarchs and deacons.
10. The day when they departed on the road, I prepared for war the armies of my patience, host after host.

11. When my soul reached the throat (i.e. when I was at the point of death), I besought that Beauty and that Grace to grant me relief,
12. And she yielded—may God preserve us from her evil, and may the victorious king repel Iblis!
13. I exclaimed, when her she-camel set out to depart, 'O driver of the reddish-white camels, do not drive them away with her!'

COMMENTARY

1. 'The full-grown camels', i.e. the actions inward and outward, for they exalt the good word to Him who is throned on high, as He hath said: 'And the good deed exalts it' (Kor. xxxv, 11). 'The peacocks' mounted on them are his loved ones: he likens them to peacocks because of their beauty. The peacocks are the spirits of those actions, for no action is acceptable or good or fair until it hath a spirit consisting in the intention or desire of its doer. He compares them to birds inasmuch as they are spiritual and also for the variety of their beauty.

2. 'With murderous glances and sovereign power': he refers to the Divine wisdom which accrues to a man in his hours of solitude, and which assaults him with such violence that he is unable to behold his personality, and which exercises dominion over him.

'A Bilqis on her throne of pearls': he refers to that which was manifested to Gabriel and to the Prophet during his night journey upon the bed of pearl and jacinth in the terrestrial heaven, when Gabriel alone swooned by reason of his knowledge of Him who manifested Himself on that occasion. The author calls the Divine wisdom 'Bilqis' on account of its being the child of theory, which is subtle, and practice, which is gross, just as Bilqis was both spirit and woman, since her father was of the Jinn and her mother was of mankind.

3. The mention of Idris alludes to her lofty and exalted rank. 'In the bosom of Idris', i.e. under his control, in respect of his turning her wheresoever he will, as the Prophet said: 'Do you bestow wisdom on those who are unworthy of it, lest ye do it a wrong.' The opposite case is that of one who speaks because he is dominated by his feeling, and who is therefore under the control of an influence. In this verse the author calls attention to his puissance in virtue of a prophetic heritage, for the prophets are masters of their spiritual feelings, whereas most of the saints are mastered by them. The sun is joined to Idris because the sun is his sphere, and the Divine wisdom is described as 'walking' (instead of 'running', etc.) because of her pride and haughtiness, and because she moves in the feelings of this heart and changes from one feeling to another with a sort of absolute power.

4. 'She kills with her glances': referring to the station of passing away in contemplation. 'Her speech restores to life': referring to the completion of the moulding of man when the spirit was breathed into him. She is compared to Jesus in reference to Kor. xxxviii, 72, 'And I breathed into him of My spirit', or Kor. xvi, 42, 'That We say to it "Be", and it is'.

5. 'Her legs': referring to Bilqis and the glass pavement (Kor. xxvii, 44).

'Is like the Tora in brightness', because the Tora is derived from the phrase, 'the stick produced fire'. The four faces of the Tora, namely, the four Books (the Koran, the Psalms, the Pentateuch, and the Gospel), correspond to the fourfold light mentioned in Kor. xxiv, 35.

6. 'One of the daughters of Rome': this wisdom, being of the race of Jesus is described as belonging to the Roman Empire. 'Unadorned', i.e. she is of the essence of unification and without any vestige of adornment from the Divine Names, yet there shines from her the 'radiance' of Absolute Goodness, viz. the burning splendours which, if God were to remove the veils of light and darkness, would consume the glories of His face.

7. 'Wild is she, none can make her his friend', because contemplation of the Essence is a passing away, in which, as as-Sayyari said, there is no pleasure. She is 'wild', inasmuch as noble souls desire to seize her, but she does not show friendship to them, because no relation exists between them and her.

'In her solitary chamber', i.e. in the heart. Her solitude is her looking on herself, for God says, 'Neither My earth nor My heaven contains Me, but I am contained by the heart of My servant who is a believer'; and since the heart which contains this essential wisdom of the race of Jesus is bare and empty of all attributes, it is like a desert and she is like a wild animal. Then he mentions the marble tomb of the Roman emperors, that such a mausoleum may remind her of death, which is the severance of union, and make her shun familiarity with the created world on account of this severance.

8. The four Books (the Koran, the Psalms, the Tora, and the Gospel) are here indicated by the mention of those who study and expound them. All the sciences comprised in the four Books point only to the Divine Names and are incapable of solving a question that concerns the Divine Essence.

9. If this spiritual being, forasmuch as she is of the race of Jesus, appeals to the Gospel by way of justifying

it in anything which men's thoughts have falsely imputed to it, we humble ourselves before her and serve her no less devotedly than do the heads of the Church, because of her majesty and sovereign might.

10. 'Upon the road', i.e. the spiritual ascension.

11. 'To grant me relief': he means what the Prophet meant by his saying, 'Lo, the breath of the Merciful comes to me from the quarter of al-Yaman.' The writer begs that the world of breaths may continually be wafted from her to him along with the spiritual feelings. The Arabs refer to this in their poetry, for they speak of giving greetings and news to be delivered by the winds when they blow.

12. 'May God preserve us from her evil!' He refers to the Tradition 'I take refuge with Thee from Thyself.'

'The victorious king', i.e. thoughts of knowledge and Divine guidance.

'Iblis', i.e. the thought of becoming one with God, for this is a hard station, and few who attain to it escape from the doctrines of an incarnation. It is the station indicated in the Tradition, 'I am his ear and his eye', etc.

13. He says, 'When this spiritual essence desired to quit this noble heart on account of its (the heart's) return from the station denoted by the words, "I have an hour which I share with none save my Lord," to the task imposed upon it of presiding over the phenomenal worlds, for which purpose its gaze is directed towards the Divine Names, the lofty aspiration on which this spiritual essence was borne to the heart, took its departure.' He calls this aspiration 'her she-camel', and the drivers of such aspirations are the angels who approach nearest to God.

V

1. My longing sought the Upland and my affliction the Lowland, so that I was between Najd and Tihama.
2. They are two contraries which cannot meet: hence my disunion will never be repaired.
3. What am I to do? What shall I devise? Guide me O my censor, do not affright me with blame!
4. Sighs have risen aloft and tears are pouring over my cheeks.
5. The camels, footsore from the journey, long for their homes and utter the plaintive cry of the frenzied lover.
6. After they have gone, my life is naught but annihilation. Farewell to it and to patience!

COMMENTARY

1. 'The Upland', referring to God on His throne.

2. 'They are two contraries', etc.: he says, 'Inasmuch as the spiritual element in man is always governing the body, it can never contemplate that which is uncomposed apart from its body and independently, as some Sufis and philosophers and ignorant persons declare.' Hence the writer says, 'my disunion will never be repaired', i.e., 'I cannot become united with Him who is pure and simple, and who resembles my essence and reality. Therefore longing is folly, for this station is unattainable, but longing is a necessary attribute of love, and accordingly I cease not from longing.'

3. 'My censor', i.e. the blaming soul.

5. 'The camels', i.e. the actions or the lofty thoughts—since, in my opinion, such thoughts belong to the class of actions—on which the good words mount to the throne of God. They 'long for their homes', i.e. for the

Divine Names from which they proceeded and by which they are controlled.

6. 'My life is naught but annihilation': he says, 'When the lofty thoughts ascend to their goal I remain in the state of passing away from passing away, for I have gained the life imperishable which is not followed by any opposite.' Accordingly, he bids farewell to patience and to the mortal life, because he has quitted the sensible world.

VI

1. When they departed, endurance and patience departed. They departed, although they were dwelling in the core of my heart.
2. I asked them where the travellers rested at noon, and I was answered, 'Their noonday resting-place is where the *shih* and the *ban* trees diffuse a sweet scent.'
3. Then I said to the wind, 'Go and overtake them, for they are biding in the shade of the grove,
4. And bear to them a greeting from a sorrowful man in whose heart are sorrows because he is separated from his people.'

COMMENTARY

1. 'They departed', i.e. the Divine Ideas. 'They were dwelling in the core of my heart': the Divine Ideas have no relationship except with their object, which is God; and God dwells in the heart, according to the Tradition 'Neither My earth nor My heaven contains Me, but I am contained in the heart of My servant who believes.' Since, however, no manifestation was vouchsafed to him at this moment, the Ideas, being objects of vision,

disappeared, notwithstanding that God was in his heart.

2. 'I asked them', i.e. the gnostics and the real existences of the past Shaykhs who were my guides on the mystic Way.

'Their noonday resting-place', etc., i.e. they reposed in every heart where the signs of longing appeared, for *shih* denotes inclination (*mayl*) and *ban* absence (*bu'd*).

3. 'I said to the wind', i.e. I sent a sign of longing after them in the hope of causing them to return to me.

'In the shade of the grove', i.e. amongst the *arak* trees, whereof the wood is used as a tooth-stick. He refers to the Tradition 'The use of the tooth-stick purifies the mouth and pleases the Lord', i.e. the Divine Ideas are dwelling in the abode of purity.

VII

1. As I kissed the Black Stone, friendly women thronged around me; they came to perform the circumambulation with veiled faces.
2. They uncovered the (faces like) sunbeams and said to me, 'Beware! for the death of the soul is in thy looking at us.
3. How many aspiring souls have we killed already at al-Muhassab of Mina, beside the pebble-heaps,
4. And in Sarhat al-Wadi and the mountains of Rama and Jam' and at the dispersion from 'Arafat!
5. Dost not thou see that beauty robs him who hath modesty, and therefore it is called the robber of virtues?
6. Our trysting-place after the circumambulation is at Zamzam beside the midmost tent, beside the rocks.
7. There everyone whom anguish hath emanciated is restored to health by the love-desire that perfumed women stir in him.

8. When they are afraid they let fall their hair, so that they are hidden by their tresses as it were by robes of darkness.'

COMMENTARY

1. 'As I kissed the Black Stone', i.e. when the Holy Hand was outstretched to me that I might take upon it the Divine oath of allegiance, referring to the verse 'Those who swear fealty to thee swear fealty to God; the hand of God is over their hands' (Kor. xlviii, 10).

'Friendly women', i.e. the angels who go round the throne of God (Kor. xxxix, 75).

2. 'The death of the soul', etc.: these spirits say, 'Do not look at us, lest thou fall passionately in love with us. Thou wert created for God, not for us, and if thou wilt be veiled by us from Him, He will cause thee to pass away from thy existence through Him, and thou wilt perish.'

3. 'Have we killed', i.e. spirits like unto us, for the above-mentioned angels who go round the Throne have no relationship except with pilgrims circumambulating the Ka'ba.

5. 'Beauty robs him who hath modesty', since the vision of Beauty enraptures whosoever beholds it.

'The robber of virtues', i.e. it takes away all delight in the vision of beauty from him who acts at the bidding of the possessor of this beauty; and sometimes the beauteous one bids thee to do that which stands between thee and glorious things, inasmuch as those things are gained by means of hateful actions: the Tradition declares that Paradise is encompassed by things which thou dislikest.

6. 'At Zamzam', i.e. in the station of the life which thou yearnest for.

'Beside the midmost tent', i.e. the intermediate world which divides the spiritual from the corporeal world.

'Beside the rocks', i.e. the sensible bodies in which the holy spiritual beings take their abode. He means that these spirits in these imaginary forms are metaphorical and transient, for they vanish from the dreamer as soon as he wakes and from the seer as soon as he returns to his senses. He warns thee not to be deceived by the manifestations of phenomenal beauty, inasmuch as all save God is unreal, i.e. not-being like unto thyself; therefore be His that He may be thine.

7. In the intermediate world whosoever loves these spiritual beings dwelling in sensible bodies derives refreshment from the world of breaths and scents because the spirit and the form are there united, so that the delight is double.

8. When these phantoms are afraid that their absoluteness will be limited by their confinement in forms, they cause thee to perceive that they are a veil which hides something more subtle than what thou seest, and conceal themselves from thee and quit these forms and once more enjoy infinite freedom.

XVI

1. They (the women) mounted the howdahs on the swift camels and placed in them the (damsels like) marble statues and full moons,
2. And promised my heart that they should return; but do the fair promise anything except deceit?
3. And she saluted with her henna-tipped fingers for the leave-taking, and let fall tears that excited the flames (of desire).
4. When she turned her back with the purpose of making for al-Khawarnaq and as-Sadir.

5. I cried out after them, 'Perdition!' She answered and said, 'Dost thou invoke perdition?
6. Then invoke it not only once, but cry "Perdition!" many times.'
7. O dove of the *arak* trees, have a little pity on me! for parting only increased thy moans,
8. And thy lamentation, O dove, inflames the longing lover, excites the jealous,
9. Melts the heart, drives off sleep, and doubles our desires and sighing.
10. Death hovers because of the dove's lamentation, and we beg him to spare us a little while,
11. That perchance a breath from the zephyr of Hajir may sweep towards us rain-clouds,
12. By means of which thou wilt satisfy thirsty souls; but thy clouds only flee farther than before.
13. O watcher of the star, be my boon-companion, and O wakeful spy on the lightning, be my nocturnal comrade!
14. O sleeper in the night, thou didst welcome sleep and inhabit the tombs ere thy death.
15. But hadst thou been in love with the fond maiden, thou wouldst have gained, through her, happiness and joy,
16. Giving to the fair (women) the wines of intimacy, conversing secretly with the suns, and flattering the full moons.

COMMENTARY

1. 'The camels' are the human faculties, 'the howdahs' are the actions which they are charged to perform, 'the damsels' in the howdahs are the mystical sciences and the perfect sorts of knowledge.

3. He says, 'This Divine subtlety, being acquired and

not given directly, is subject to a change produced by contact with phenomena'; this change he indicates by speaking of 'her henna-tipped fingers', as though it were the modification of unity by a kind of association. Nevertheless, her staying in the heart is more desirable than her going, for she protects the gnostic as long as she is there.

'And let fall tears', etc.: she let loose in the heart sciences of contemplation which produced an intense yearning.

4. 'Al-Khawarnaq and as-Sadir', i.e. the Divine presence.

5. 'Perdition!' i.e. death to the phenomenal world now that these sublime mysteries have vanished from it.

'Dost thou invoke perdition?' i.e. why dost thou not see the face of God in everything, in light and darkness, in simple and composite, in subtle and gross, in order that thou mayst not feel the grief of parting.

6. 'Cry "Perdition!" many times' (cf. Kor. xxv, 15), i.e. not only in this station but in every station in which thou art placed, for thou must bid farewell to every one of them, and thou canst not fail to be grieved, since, whenever the form of the Truth disappears from thee, thou imaginest that He has left thee; but He has not left thee, and it is only thy remaining with thyself that veils from thee the vision of that which pervades the whole of creation.

7. 'O dove of the *arak* trees': he addresses holy influences of Divine pleasure which have descended upon him.

'Have a little pity on me!' i.e. pity my weakness and inability to attain unto thy purity.

'For parting only increased thy moans': he says, 'Inasmuch as thy substance only exists through and in me, and I am diverted from thee by the dark world of phenomena which keeps me in bondage, for this cause thou art lamenting thy separation from me.'

8. 'And thy lamentation', etc., i.e. we who seek the unbounded freedom of the celestial world should weep more bitterly than thou.

'Excites the jealous': jealousy arises from regarding others, and he who beholds God in everything feels no jealousy, for God is One; but since God manifests Himself in various forms, the term 'jealousy' is applicable to Him.

10. 'Death', i.e. the station in which the subtle principle of Man is severed from its governance of this dark body for the sake of the Divine subtleties which are conveyed to it by the above-mentioned holy influences.

11. 'Hajir' denotes here the most inaccessible veil of the Divine glory. No phenomenal being can attain to the immediate experience thereof, but scents of it blow over the hearts of gnostics in virtue of a kind of amorous affection.

'Rain-clouds', i.e. sciences and diverse sorts of knowledge belonging to the most holy Essence.

13. 'O watcher of the star', in reference to keeping in mind that which the sciences offer in their various connexions.

'O wakeful spy on the lightning': the lightning is a *locus* of manifestation of the Essence. The author says, addressing one who seeks it, 'Our quest is the same, be my comrade in the night.'

14. This verse may be applied either to the heedless or to the unconscious.

15. 'The fond maiden', i.e. the Essential subtlety which is the gnostic's object of desire.

'Through her': although She is unattainable, yet hrough her manifestation to thee all that thou hast is baptized for thee, and thy whole kingdom is displayed to thee by that Essential form.

16. 'Conversing secretly with the suns', etc., in reference to the Traditions which declare that God will be seen in the next world like the sun in a cloudless sky or like the moon when she is full.

XX

1. My lovesickness is from her of the lovesick eyelids: console me by the mention of her, console me!
2. The grey doves fluttered in the meadows and wailed: the grief of these doves is from that which grieved me.
3. May my father be the ransom of a tender playful girl, one of the maidens guarded in howdahs, advancing swayingly among the married women!
4. She rose, plain to see, like a sun, and when she vanished she shone in the horizon of my heart.
5. O ruined abodes at Rama! How many fair damsels with swelling breasts have they beheld!
6. May my father and I myself be the ransom of a God-nurtured gazelle which pastures between my ribs in safety!
7. The fire thereof in that place is light: thus is the light the quencher of the fires.
8. O my two friends, bend my reins aside that I may see the form of her abode with clear vision.
9. And when ye reach the abode, descend, and there, my two companions, weep for me,
10. And stop with me a little while at the ruins, that we may endeavour to weep, nay, that I may weep indeed because of that which befell me.
11. Passion shoots me without arrows, passion slays me without a spear.

12. Tell me, will ye weep with me when I weep beside her? Help me, oh help me to weep!
13. And rehearse to me the tale of Hind and Lubna and Sulayma and Zaynab and 'Inan!
14. Then tell me further of Hajir and Zarus, give me news of the pastures of the gazelles!
15. And mourn for me with the poetry of Qays and Lubna, and with Mayya and the afflicted Ghaylan!
16. Long have I yearned for a tender maiden, endowed with prose and verse, having a pulpit, eloquent,
17. One of the princesses from the land of Persia, from the most glorious of cities, from Isfahan.
18. She is the daughter of 'Iraq, the daughter of my Imam, and I am her opposite, a child of Yemen.
19. O my lords, have ye seen or heard that two opposites are ever united!
20. Had you seen us at Rama proffering each other cups of passion without fingers,
21. Whilst passion caused sweet and joyous words to be uttered us without a tongue,
22. You would have seen a state in which the understanding disappears—Yemen and 'Iraq embracing together.
23. Falsely spoke the poet who said before my time (and he has pelted me with the stones of his understanding),
24. 'O thou who givest the Pleiades in marriage to Suhayl, God bless thee! how should they meet?
25. The Pleiades are in the north whenever they rise, and Suhayl whenever he rises is in the south.'

COMMENTARY

1. 'Her of the lovesick eyelids': he means the Presence

desired by gnostics. Although she is too sublime to be known and loved, she inclines toward them in mercy and kindness and descends into their hearts by a sort of manifestation.

'Console me by the mention of her': there is no cure for his malady but remembrance. He says 'Console me' twice, i.e. by my remembrance of God and by God's remembrance of me (cf. Kor. ii, 147).

2. 'The grey doves', i.e. the spirits of the intermediate world.

'And wailed', because their souls cannot join the spirits which have been released from imprisonment in this earthly body.

3. 'A tender playful girl', i.e. a form of Divine wisdom, essential and holy, which fills the heart with joy.

'One of the maidens guarded in howdahs': she is a virgin, because none has ever known her before; she was veiled in modesty and jealousy during all her journey from the Divine Presence to the heart of this gnostic.

'The married women', i.e. the forms of Divine wisdom already realized by gnostics who preceded him.

4. 'And when she vanished', etc., i.e. when she set in the world of evidence she rose in the world of the Unseen.

5. 'O ruined abodes', i.e. the bodily faculties.

'At Rama', from (he sought), implying that their search is vain.

'How many fair damsels', etc., i.e. subtle and Divine forms by which the bodily faculties were annihilated.

7. The natural fires are extinguished by the heavenly light in his heart.

8. 'The form of her abode', i.e. the Presence from which she issued forth. He seems to desire the station of Divine contemplation, since wisdom is not desired

except for the sake of that to which it leads.

9. 'Weep for me', because this Presence annihilates everyone who attains unto her and beholds her.

10. 'That I may weep', etc., i.e. for the loss of the loved ones and of everything except the ruins of their abode.

11. 'Without arrows', i.e. from a distance.

12. 'Without a spear', i.e. near at hand.

13. Hind was the mistress of Bishr, and Lubna of Qays b. al-Dharih; 'Inan was a slave-girl belonging to an-Natifi; Zaynab was one of the mistresses of 'Umar b. Abi Rabi'a; Sulayma was a slave girl whom the author had seen: he says that she had a lover. He interprets the names of all these women mystically, e.g. Hind is explained as an allusion to the Fall of Adam, and Zaynab as signifying removal from the station of saintship to that of prophecy.

16. He describes this essential knowledge as endowed with prose and verse, i.e. absolute in respect of her essence, but limited in respect of possession.

'A pulpit', i.e. the ladder of the Most Beautiful Names. To climb this ladder is to be invested with the qualitites of these Names.

'Eloquent', referring to the station of Apostleship.

The author adds: 'I allude enigmatically to the various kinds of mystical knowledge which are under the veil of an-Nizam, the maiden daughter of our Shaykh.'

17. 'One of the princesses', on account of her asceticism, for ascetics are the kings of the earth.

18. ''Iraq' indicates origin, i.e. this knowledge comes of a noble race.

'A child of Yemen', i.e. in respect of faith and wisdom and the breath of the Merciful and tenderness of heart. These qualities are the opposite of what is attributed to 'Iraq, viz. rudeness and severity and infidelity, whereas the opposite of 'Iraq itself is not Yemen, but the Maghrib, and the opposite of Yemen itself is not 'Iraq, but Syria. The antithesis here is between the qualities of the Beloved and those of the lover.

19. 'Two opposites', referring to the story of Junayd, when a man sneezed in his presence and said, 'God be praised!' (Kor. i, 1). Junayd said, completing the verse, 'Who is the Lord of created beings.' The man replied, 'And who is the created being, that he should be mentioned in the same breath with God?' 'O my brother,' said Junayd, 'the phenomenal, when it is joined to the Eternal, vanishes and leaves no trace behind. When He is there, thou art not, and if thou art there, He is not.'

22. 'Yemen and 'Iraq', etc., i.e. the identification of the qualities of Wrath and Mercy. He refers to the saying of Abu Sa'id al-Kharraz, who on being asked how he knew God, answered, 'By His uniting two opposites, for He is the First and the Last and the Outward and the Inward' (Kor. lvii, 3).

24. 'The Pleiades', i.e. the seven attributes demonstrated by scholastic philosophers.

'Suhayl', i.e. the Divine Essence.

25. 'In the north', i.e. in the world of phenomena. The Divine attributes are manifested in Creation, but the Divine Essence does not enter into Creation.

XXVIII

1. Between al-Naqa and La'la' are the gazelles of
   Dhat al-Ajra',
2. Grazing there in a dense covert of tangled shrubs,
   and pasturing.
3. New moons never rose on the horizon of that hill
4. But I wished, from fear, that they had not risen.

5. And never appeared a flash from the lightning of that fire-stone
6. But I desired, for my feeling's sake, that it had not flashed.
7. O my tears, flow! O mine eye, cease not to shed tears!
8. O my sighs, ascend! O my heart, split!
9. And thou, O camel-driver, go slowly, for the fire is between my ribs.
10. From their copious flow through fear of parting my tears have all been spent,
11. So that, when the time of starting comes, thou wilt not find an eye to weep.
12. Set forth, then, to the valley of the curving sands, their abode and my death-bed——
13. There are those whom I love, beside the waters of al-Ajraʿ——
14. And call to them, 'Who will help a youth burning with desire, one dismissed,
15. Whose sorrows have thrown him into a bewilderment which is the last remnant of ruin?
16. O moon beneath a darkness, take from him something and leave something,
17. And bestow on him a glance from behind yonder veil,
18. Because he is too weak to apprehend the terrible beauty,
19. Or flatter him with hopes, that perchance he may be revived or may understand.
20. He is a dead man between al-Naqa and Laʿlaʿ.
21. For I am dead of despair and anguish, as though I were fixed in my place.
22. The East Wind did not tell the truth when it brought cheating phantoms.
23. Sometimes the wind deceives when it causes thee to hear what is not (really) heard.

1. 'Between al-Naqa and La'la', etc., i.e. between the hill of white musk, on which is the vision of God, and the place of frenzied love for Him, are diverse sorts of knowledge connected with the stations of abstraction.

2. 'In a dense covert of tangled shrubs', i.e. the world of phenomenal admixture and interdependence.

3. 'New moons', i.e. Divine manifestations.

4. 'From fear', i.e. from fear that the beholder might pass away in himself from himself, and that his essence might perish, whereas his object is to continue subsistent through God and for God; or from fear that he should imagine the manifestation to be according to the essential nature of God in Himself (which is impossible), and not according to the nature of the recipient. The former belief, which involves the comprehension of God by the person to whom the manifestation is made, agrees with the doctrine of some speculative theologians, who maintain that our knowledge of God and Gabriel's knowledge of Him and His knowledge of Himself are the same. How far is this from the truth!

5. 'A flash from the lightning of that fire-stone', i.e. an inanimate, phenomenal, and earthly manifestation.

9. 'O camel-driver', i.e. the voice of God calling the aspirations to Himself.

'The fire', i.e. the fire of Love.

10-11. He says that his eyes have been melted away by the tears which he shed in anticipation of parting.

12. 'To the valley of the curving sands', i.e. the station of mercy and tenderness.

'My death-bed', because the Divine mercy causes him to pass away in bewilderment.

13. 'Beside the waters of al-Ajra': because this mercy is the result of painful self-mortification.

14. 'One dismissed', i.e. one who has come to himself again after contemplation, according to the tradition that God says, after having shown Himself to His servants in Paradise, 'Send them back to their pavilions.'

16. 'A darkness', i.e. the forms in which the manifestation takes place.

'Take from him something', etc., i.e. take from him whatever is related to himself, and leave whatever is not related to himself, so that only the Divine Spirit may remain in him.

21. 'For I am dead of despair and anguish', i.e. I despair of attaining the reality of that which I seek, and I grieve for the time spent in a vain search for it.

'As though I were fixed in my place', i.e. I cannot escape from my present state, inasmuch as it is without place, quantity, and quality, being purely transcendental.

22. 'Cheating phantoms', i.e. the similes and images in which God, who has no like, is presented to us by the world of breaths.

XXIX

1. May my father be the ransom of the boughs swaying to and fro as they bend, bending their tresses towards the cheeks!
2. Loosing plaited locks of hair; soft in their joints and bends;
3. Trailing skirts of haughtiness; clad in embroidered garments of beauty;
4. Which from modesty grudge to bestow their loveliness; which give old heirlooms and new gifts;
5. Which charm by their laughing and smiling mouths; whose lips are sweet to kiss;

6. Whose bare limbs are dainty; which have swelling breasts and offer choice presents;
7. Luring ears and souls, when they converse, by their wondrous witchery;
8. Covering their faces for shame, taking captive thereby the devout and fearing heart;
9. Displaying teeth like pearls, healing with their saliva one who is feeble and wasted;
10. Darting from their eyes glances which pierce a heart experienced in the wars and used to combat;
11. Making rise from their bosoms new moons which suffer no eclipse on becoming full;
12. Causing tears to flow as from rain-clouds, causing sighs to be heard like the crash of thunder.
13. O my two comrades, may my life-blood be the ransom of a slender girl who bestowed on me favours and bounties!
14. She established the harmony of union, for she is our principle of harmony: she is both Arab and foreign; she makes the gnostic forget.
15. Whenever she gazes, she draws against thee trenchant swords, and her front teeth show to thee a dazzling levin.
16. O my comrades, halt beside the guarded pasture of Hajir! Halt, halt, O my comrades,
17. That I may ask where their camels have turned, for I have plunged into places of destruction and death,
18. And scenes known to me and unknown, with a swift camel which complains of her worn hoofs and of deserts and wildernesses,
19. A camel whose flanks are lean and whose rapid journeying caused her to lose her strength and the fat of her hump,

20. Until I brought her to a halt in the sandy tract of Hajir and saw she-camels followed by young ones at al-Uthayl.

21. They were led by a moon of awful mien, and I clasped him to my ribs for fear that he should depart,

22. A moon that appeared in the circumambulation, and while he circumambulated me I was not circumambulating anyone except him.

23. He was effacing his footprints with the train of his robe, so that thou wouldst be bewildered even if thou wert the guide tracing out his track.

COMMENTARY

1. 'My father', i.e. Universal Reason.

'The boughs', i.e. the Attributes which bear Divine knowledge to gnostics and mercifully incline towards them.

2. 'Locks of hair', i.e. hidden sciences and mysteries. They are called 'plaited' in allusion to the various degrees of knowledge.

'Soft', in respect of their graciously inclining to us.

'In their joints and bends', in reference to the conjunction of real and phenomenal qualities.

3. 'Trailing skirts', etc., because of the loftiness of their rank.

'Clad in embroidered garments', etc., i.e. appearing in diverse beautiful shapes.

4. 'Which from modesty', etc., referring to the Tradition, 'Do not bestow wisdom except on those who are worthy of it, lest ye do it a wrong', since contemplation is not vouchsafed to everyone.

'Old heirlooms', i.e. knowledge demonstrated by proofs derived from another.

'New gifts', i.e. knowledge of which the proof is bestowed by God and occurs to one's own mind as the result of sound reflection.

8. 'Covering their faces for shame', i.e. they are ashamed to reveal themselves to those whose hearts are generally occupied with something other than God, viz. the ordinary believers described in Kor. ix, 103.

9. 'Teeth like pearls', i.e. the sciences of Divine majesty.

10. 'Experienced in the wars', etc., i.e. able to distinguish the real from the phenomenal in the similitudes presented to the eye.

11. 'From their bosoms', i.e. from the Divine attributes.

'New moons', i.e. a manifestation in the horizon.

'Which suffer no eclipse', i.e. they are not subject to any natural lust that veils them from the Divine Ideas.

13. 'A slender girl', i.e. the single, subtle, and essential knowledge of God.

14. 'She established the harmony of union', i.e. this knowledge concentrated me upon myself and united me with my Lord.

'Arab', i.e. it caused me to know myself from myself.

'Foreign', i.e. it caused me to know myself from God, because the Divine knowledge is synthetic and does not admit of analysis except by means of comparison; and since comparison is impossible, therefore analysis is impossible; whence it follows that synthesis also is impossible, and I only use the latter term in order to convey to the reader's intelligence a meaning that is not to be apprehended save by immediate feeling and intuition.

'Forget', i.e. his knowledge and himself.

15. 'A dazzling levin', i.e. a manifestation of the Essence in the state of beauty and joy.

16. 'O my comrades': he means his understanding and his faith.

17. 'Their camels', i.e. the aspirations which carry the sciences and subtle essences of man to their goal.

18. 'A swift camel', i.e. an aspiration in himself.

19. 'Whose rapid journeying', etc., i.e. this aspiration was connected with many aspects of plurality which disappeared in the course of its journey towards Unity.

20. 'In the sandy tract of Hajir', i.e. a state which enabled me to discriminate between phenomena and prevented me from regarding anything except what this state revealed to me.

'She-camels followed by young ones', i.e. original sciences from which other sciences are derived.

21. 'A moon of awful mien', i.e. a manifestation of Divine majesty in the heart.

23. 'His footprints', i.e. the evidences which He adduced as a clue to Himself.

'The train of his robe', i.e. His uniqueness and incomparability.

'So that thou wouldst be bewildered', i.e. our knowledge of Him is ignorance and bewilderment and helplessness. He says that in order that gnostics may recognize the limits of their knowledge of God.

XLIX

1. Who will show me her of the dyed fingers? Who will
 show me her of the honeyed tongue?
2. She is one of the girls with swelling breasts who
 guard their honour, tender, virgin, and beautiful.
3. Full moons over branches: they fear no waning.
4. In a garden of my body's country is a dove perched
 on a *ban* bough,

5. Dying of desire, melting with passion, because that which befell me hath befallen her;
6. Mourning for a mate, blaming Time, who shot her unerringly, as he shot me.
7. Parted from a neighbour and far from a home! Alas, in my time of severance, for my time of union!
8. Who will bring me her who is pleased with my torment? I am helpless because of that with which she is pleased.

COMMENTARY

1. 'Her of the dyed fingers': he means the phenomenal power by which the Eternal power is hidden according to the doctrine of some scholastic theologians. He says, 'Who will impart to me the truth of this matter, so far as knowledge thereof is possible?' He wishes to know whether God manifests Himself therein or not. The author denies such manifestation, but some mystics and the Mu'tazilites allow it, while the Sufis among the Ash'arites leave the question undecided.

4. 'A dove', etc., i.e. a spiritual Prophetic essence which appeared in the incommunicable self-subsistence. He refers to the belief of some Sufis that Man cannot be invested with the Divine Self-subsistence.

5. 'Dying of desire', etc., with reference to Kor. iii, 29, '*Follow me, that God may love you,*' and Kor. v, 59, '*He loves them and they love Him.*'

6. 'A mate', i.e. the Universal Form.

'Blaming Time,' because the forms belonging to the world of similitude are limited by Time in that world.

7. 'A neighbour', i.e. a gnostic who became veiled

from his Lord by his 'self' after having subsisted by his Lord and for the sake of his Lord.

'A home,' i.e. his natural constitution, whenever he returns to it.

LVIII

1. Oh, is there any way to the damsels bright and fair? And is there anyone who will show me their traces?
2. And can I halt at night beside the tents of the curving sand? And can I rest at noon in the shade of the *arak* trees?
3. The tongue of inward feeling spoke, informing me that she says, 'Wish for that which is attainable.'
4. My love for thee is whole, O thou end of my hopes, and because of that love my heart is sick.
5. Thou art exalted, a full moon rising over the heart, a moon that never sets after it hath risen.
6. May I be thy ransom, O thou who art glorious in beauty and pride! for thou hast no equal amongst the fair.
7. Thy gardens are wet with dew and thy roses are blooming, and thy beauty is passionately loved: it is welcome to all.
8. Thy flowers are smiling and thy boughs are fresh: wherever they bend, the winds bend towards them.
9. Thy grace is tempting and thy look piercing: armed with it the knight, affliction, rushes upon me.

COMMENTARY

1. 'The damsels bright and fair', i.e. the knowledge derived from the manifestations of His Beautiful Name.

2. 'The tents of the curving sand', i.e. the stations of Divine favour.

'The shade of the *arak* trees', i.e. contemplation of the pure and holy Presence.

3. This station is gained only by striving and sincere application, not by wishing. 'Travel that thou mayst attain.'

5. 'A moon that never sets', etc.: he points out that God never manifests Himself to anything and then becomes veiled from it afterwards.

7. 'Thy gardens are wet with dew', i.e. all Thy creatures are replenished by the Divine qualities which are revealed to them.

'Thy roses are blooming', in reference to a particular manifestation which destroys every blameworthy quality.

'It is welcome', i.e. it is loved for its essence.

8. 'Thy flowers', etc., i.e. Thy knowledge is welcome to the heart.

'Thy boughs', i.e. the spiritual influences which convey Thy knowledge.

LIX

1. Tayba hath a gazelle from whose witching eye (glances like) the edge of a keen blade are drawn,
2. And at 'Arafat I perceived what she desired and I was not patient,
3. And on the night of Jam' we had union with her, such as is mentioned in the proverb.
4. The girl's oath is false: do not confide in that which betrays.
5. The wish I gained at Mina, would that it might continue to the last hour of my life!

6. In La'la' I was transported with love for her who displays to thee the splendour of the bright moon.
7. She shot Rama and inclined to dalliance at as-Saba and removed the interdiction at al-Hajir.
8. And she watched a lightning-gleam over Bariq with a glance swifter than a thought that passes in the mind.
9. And the waters of al-Ghada were diminished by a blazing fire which passion kindled within his ribs.
10. And she appeared at the *ban* tree of an-Naqa and chose (for her adornment) the choicest of its superb hidden pearls.
11. And at Dhat al-Ada she turned backward in dread of the lurking lion.
12. At Dhu Salam she surrendered my life-blood to her murderous languishing glance.
13. She stood on guard at the guarded pasture and bent at the sand-bend, swayed by all-cancelling decisive resolution.
14. And at 'Alij she managed her affair (in such a way) that she might escape from the claw of the bird.
15. Her Khawarnaq rends the sky and towers beyond the vision of the observer.

COMMENTARY

1. 'Tayba (Medina) hath a gazelle', referring to a Muhammadan degree, i.e. a spiritual presence belonging to the station of Muhammad.

3. 'On the night of Jam'': he says, 'we abode in the station of proximity and He concentrated me upon myself.'

'In the proverb', namely, 'He did not salute until he bade farewell' i.e. they parted as soon as they met.

4. He says, 'Put no trust in an Attribute that is not self-subsistent and depends on One who may not always accomplish its desires.'

7. 'She shot Rama,' i.e. she shot that which she was seeking, because she regarded the thing as being the opposite of what it was and of what she believed it to be.

'And inclined to dalliance at as-Saba', i.e. she desired to manifest herself.

8. 'A lightning-gleam', i.e. a *locus* of manifestation for the Essence.

10. 'And chose', etc., i.e. she revealed herself in the most lovely shape.

11. 'Dhat al-Ada', i.e. the place of illumination.

'She turned backward', etc., i.e. she returned to her natural world for fear that that fierce light should consume her.

12. Gnostics are annihilated by their vision of the Truth, but this does not happen to the vulgar, because they lack knowledge of themselves.

13. 'The guarded pasture', i.e. the station of Divine glory. 'Bent', i.e. inclined with Divine mercy. This refers to her investing herself with Divine qualities.

14. 'That she might escape', etc., i.e. she was unwilling to receive from the spirits, for she wished to receive only from God, by intuitive feeling, not by cognition. God sometimes bestows His gifts by the mediation of the exalted spirits, and sometimes immediately.

15. 'Her Khawarnaq', i.e. the seat of her kingdom.

LX

1. Approach the dwelling of dear ones who have taken covenants—may clouds of incessant rain pour upon it!——

2. And breathe the scent of the wind over against their land, in desire that the (sweet) airs may tell thee where they are.
3. I know that they encamped at the *ban* tree of Idam, where the *arar* plants grow and the *shih* and the *katam*.

COMMENTARY

1. 'Dear ones', i.e. the exalted spirits.

'Covenants,' i.e. the Divine covenants taken from the spirits of the prophets.

'Clouds of incessant rain', i.e. knowledge descending upon them continuously.

2. 'And breathe', etc., referring to the Tradition, 'I feel the breath of the Merciful from the quarter of Yemen.'

3. 'At the *ban* tree of Idam', i.e. the station of Absolute purity at the end of the journey to God.

'The *arar* plants', etc., i.e. sweet spiritual influences proceeding from lovely spiritual beings.

INDEX

GEORGE ALLEN & UNWIN LTD
London: 40 Museum Street, W.C.1

Auckland: 24 Wyndham Street
Bombay: 15 Graham Road, Ballard Estate, Bombay 1
Calcutta: 17 Chittaranjan Avenue, Calcutta 13
Cape Town: 109 Long Street
Karachi: Metherson's Estate, Wood Street, Karachi 2
New Delhi: 13–14 Ajmeri Gate Extension, New Delhi 1
São Paulo: Avenida 9 de Julho 1138–Ap. 51
Singapore, South East Asia and Far East, 36c, Prinsep Street
Sydney, N.S.W.: Bradbury House, 55 York Street
Toronto: 91 Wellington Street West

Lightning Source UK Ltd.
Milton Keynes UK
UKOW06f0648110714

234949UK00008B/88/P

9 781295 817245